ONE EIGHTYSEVEN
A DAY IN THE LIFE

DEREK GROVER

author HOUSE

AuthorHouse™
1663 Liberty Drive
Bloomington, IN 47403
www.authorhouse.com
Phone: 833-262-8899

Published by AuthorHouse 12/03/2024

ISBN: 979-8-8230-3061-8 (sc)
ISBN: 979-8-8230-3062-5 (e)

Library of Congress Control Number: 2024916966

Print information available on the last page.

Contents

I dedicate this book to my dead son Derek Grover II and the people I left behind in San Diego's George Baily Detention Facility. No one can tell you to stop being in a gang but when you're ready please stop.

Introduction

They kept laughing and joking, before I walked into the courtroom the deputy told me, Grover, you better not try to speak to anyone you know. He said, if I did, he was going to take them out the courtroom. Everyone behind me started to talk louder. I turned to the deputy and said, deputy, can you take me out the courtroom now?

Chapter 1

SO WHY AM I GOING TO JAIL

It was just another Tuesday.
Laundry day. Shoving my pile of faded
clothes into the washer left me with
zero options. The familiar blue outfit
it was again. Today, this outfit felt
more like a uniform a jail uniform.

As I puffed on a blunt on my way
home, rounding the corner in Encanto
like I always did, my world went
sideways. San Diego Police Department.
Three squad cars, two undercover
vehicles, and a K-9 unit all for me.

It was about to be a foot chase
for the history books. Too late. I
found myself sprawled on the hood
of a marked police car. "Hold on," I

barked. "Before you barge in my house, announce yourselves! Police!" The lead officer heeded my warning. A collective sigh of relief rippled through the air as they finally lowered their guns from my head.

Handcuffed and leaning against the squad car, I could still hear the murmurs: "D-Man..." "What the hell were you thinking when you shot up Morse High School?"

"Man, to tell you the truth, I don't know what the hell I was thinking. All I know is I just got up and went to kill somebody."

"I was driving down Skyline, and I saw two hundred gangsters standing on the sidewalk. I thought I could take one out."

"So, I pulled out my shotgun, a sawed-off, but nobody ran. So, I fired. Out of two hundred gang members all dressed in red, it was just my luck to bust on the police."

"I thought they were gang members. When they started shooting back at me,

I could hear bullets all around me
going 'pink, pink, pink.'"

"The police shot out all my car
windows."

"D-Man, remember when Baby Nut
killed that gangster at the stop
sign?"

"He did it for you, D-Man, the
big homie, right?" I thought it was
my gun, but he didn't do it for me.
He did it because he was deep in
gangbanging.

He wanted all the smoke, and he
found it.

Some gangsters seek out blunt
smoke, gun smoke, while others search
for smoke in the cell block. All
gangsters understand: never hit a
rival gang member in the face with
your backup lights. It'll leave you
with a hole in your head, with smoke
billowing out, just like the blunt I
was smoking.

So why am I going to jail?
You'll find out downtown at police
headquarters.

After a mugshot session at the downtown police station, I was escorted to downtown's central jail.

I spent a few hours there before being transported to San Diego's Maximum Security Jail, the George Bailey Detention Facility. It's situated next to Donovan State Prison, which lies south, adjacent to Tijuana State Prison.

In between, there's a juvenile facility for violent juvenile gang members.

In George Bailey's Super Max cell block 6B, Mexican gang members can't recline on their bunks all day.

They stay rolled up 24 hours a day.

"In George Bailey, you can't walk through the racially divided tables in the cell block; they're pointed towards Tijuana like the tip of a spear.

You might get shanked walking through someone's gang territory that leads to different hoods; it can lead to your death.

You must pay attention; this type
of disrespect will kick off a beatdown.
It is considered and will be taken as
a major threat.

Oh yeah, another thing: you can't
take a shower upstairs only whites and
Mexicans. Blacks use the mirror on the
wall downstairs. No matter what hood
you're from, you shower downstairs.

Keep in mind, in the past two
weeks, there have been two riots.

You came in just in time to tip the
scales of power."

This is a two tier cell block,
Bloods on top, Crips below.

Never let out together, of course.

Just pressed against our cell
doors, a volatile mix of bloodlust and
frustration. The cops keep us apart,
the only thing stopping a full-blown
riot.

Chill Dogg, a West Coast Crip,
sized me up when I first landed here.
"What's up, D-Man?" he rumbled.

They got me on another one, I muttered, not elaborating.

"Yeah, I saw you on KUSI News, Channel 6." Thanks Chill Dogg, for drawing everyone's attention.

He retreated, back to his cell, leaving me exposed to a sea of fifteen smirking Southsiders. Didn't faze me one bit, not with them watching my arrest play out on the day room TV.

One by one, they shuffled over, introductions laced with veiled threats. Cell 228, tier two, became my new home.

As I climbed the stairs, I couldn't help but overhear Chill Dogg briefing his twenty-strong Crip car back in his cell.

The first time I ever unleashed the fury of an AK-47 was in that niggas hood. Now, three Southsiders were moving out of cell 228, mattresses slung over their shoulders a blatant display of power by my presents.

Stepping into cell 228, the first thing I did was submit a request for the chapel. Surprisingly, it was granted. This was my prison and jail chapel debut. They asked for a testimony.

I cleared my throat. "I'm Derek Grover, also known as D-Man… THE GANGSTER CRIMINAL." My voice echoed in the chapel. "Twenty-seven years I was as a gang member." Tears welled in my eyes as I asked for forgiveness for the sins of gangbanging, for the life I'd led. But the others… they seemed lost in their own world they were staring at the faded calendar on the wall. My voice cracked.

"I can't escape it," I confessed. 5 life terms plus 50 years in gang enhancements.

Kidnapping, robbery, abduction... the list goes on.

The path I walk feels divinely ordained, with fear now a distant echo. Yet, my heart remains heavy, mourning my fallen homeboy, Killer-Bob. A shootout claimed him, going out blazing with an AK-47 against the

San Diego PD at the firing range, on Federal.

They called it "smoked." Here, in 6B, I warned anyone laughing about it that they would meet violence.

"Killer-Bob," I growled, "a modern-day gunslinger." "Another murder on my plate, fuck them," I spat. I did what I had to.

My homeboy, Sidny Bobo from Lincoln, was cut from the same cloth. In this concrete tomb, God became my only solace.

It was on the fateful day Killer-Bob died. It played out like a scene from Gunsmoke, with Matt Dillon slapping cuffs on D-Man before the showdown that took KB. They stripped everything from him that day a hundred racks, a hundred racks from the AK-47 he used to bust on them.

My prayers for freedom were finally answered, a miracle I never dared to believe. San Diego's streets, once a distant dream, were now beneath my feet. Tears, a constant companion for years, still welled up at times.

The acrid scent of gun smoke, a permanent memory. Driven by a desire for redemption, I wrote the book. When I shared this with the group, I confessed my past and expressed my love for them despite our shared history of gang violence. Yet, a question lingered: why did gangbanging feel spiritual, as if it were a twisted gift from God? "This book," I declared, "is my redemption." I signed each copy with a personal note: *"Derek Grover, aka D-Man.*

No longer the Gangster Criminal 187." My message was clear: guide the youth, teach them right from wrong. Don't sugarcoat my past; show them the harsh realities. A wave of cheers erupted. Handshakes, pats on the shoulder a sense of community I hadn't felt in years.

We closed with a prayer, a collective plea for guidance: "God, please guide us..." Thoughts of Killer-Bob, death, and the brutality of gang life swirled in my head as I returned to the cell block. Clothing exchange was underway.

This meant stripping down, our
belongings scrutinized by watchful
eyes for any contraband. Dirty clothes
were swapped for fresh ones, offering
not just a clean appearance but a
chance to reset our mindset.

The guards' warning echoed in
my mind: anything illegal found
in our cells meant no football on
Thanksgiving a harsh blow considering
the holiday's spirit. Thankfully, the
exchange went smoothly, leaving us
with clean blue and whites. Released
from lockdown, I found myself drawn
to a gangster holding court at the
"Generals table," the unofficial seat of
power.

"Where you from?" I asked, already
anticipating the answer. "Compton,
Piru," he rumbled. "Fruit Town's the
name." Around him, a dozen others
gathered, a mix of gangsters from
Skyline, Lincoln, and the Brims.
The gangsters I approached at the
"Generals table" weren't welcoming.

They surrounded me, a tightening
noose. Saying "where you from?" was
apparently an invitation I hadn't

intended. "Roll up," they snarled,
gang jargon for joining their group.
"Fuck you," I spat back, defiance
burning in my chest.

I jabbed my finger at the gangster's
face, a foolish imitation of a gun.
He flinched, backing down a step.
Not wanting to escalate further, I
swallowed the insult that would have
branded him a bitch.

"We can take it to the cell,"
I muttered, a prison term for a
contained fight. Lock yourself in, fight
it out, then wave it off to the guards
who would eventually intervene only to
pop your cell back open. Five Bloods,
led by a Lincoln gangster named
Redrum, surged into my cell, while
Fruit Town remained outside.

Redrum started his spiel, flaunting
his Blood affiliation. "This is my
house," I growled. "Leave your gang
shit at the door." The deputies,
wary of me aligning with the Crips,
stuck me right in the heart of enemy
territory the Bloods' tier.

Ironically, it was 6B, cell 228, the same one I occupied fifteen years ago when Killer-Bob died. They'd even cleared out three Southsiders to make room for me, making me a one-man target.

After the dust settled from the altercation with the Bloods in my cell, I buzzed for the door, and it opened. We all shuffled back down to tier one. I felt an undeniable pull toward the "Generals table," the unofficial seat of power. "Fruit Town," I said, my voice steely.

I'm going to knock off your boys one by one. I leaned in closer. "You ain't from San Diego, that's why you didn't step up. Out-of-town gangmembers don't fight our battles. In here, you fight for what you believe in, not someone else's hood." Alone in my cell, a chilling thought struck me: did Al-Dog follow my advice and go on the run?

That single call was all I could manage, leaving me in the dark about his fate. The silence was broken only by the relentless dripping from the broken faucet. It was a problem I

could handle, just like dealing with
Redrum a forceful fix, a jammed pencil
to silence the flow. But unlike the
faucet, Redrum wouldn't be so easily
subdued.

The irony wasn't lost on me. My
cell, a sweltering sauna thanks to
the malfunctioning faucet stuck on
scalding hot, contrasted sharply
with the icy grip of fear around
Al-Dog's fate.

Chapter 2

FACE THE DEVIL

The next morning, I requested to be a worker for the day. A worker helps keep the cell block clean, handles food from the food cart, mops, and performs other general tasks that prisoners do.

My first task was to get things set up for morning chow. It sounds simple, but this job can get you seriously fucked up. Food in this cell block is power—like gas for a car. When it's empty, you can't move; it's the same for the human body. One of the first things you do is cover your hair with a net. I'm bald, but everyone hates seeing blacks with hair, especially around their food.

Touching their stuff is even worse;
it's like leaving your fingerprints
at a robbery scene. Always wear the
plastic gloves. In this cell block,
fuckin with other prisoners' food will
put you in danger. You have to reach
into the food cart, pull out the food
tray, and hand it to each prisoner one
at a time.

It seems simple, but you need to
know that talking over other people's
food, especially if you're not from
the same race or gang, could get you
killed. "Wipe the sleep out of your
eyes and face the devil this morning.
The best way to do that is to be
prepared."

As I handed each inmate their tray,
everyone was saying, "Good looking
out, OG." I didn't respond.

I just nodded my head up and down.
Responding would mean talking over
the food, which can and will be taken
as spitting in it.

On top of that, you already have to
touch their tray, and some gangsters

hold a grudge against you for that alone.

Also, you might hand a gangster the wrong tray, maybe the meat is out of place or no cookie or your bread has been soaked from a wet tray.

Anyway, the wrong person the wrong tray and you'll pay for it.

Next you must know how to feed your people.

After everyone in the cell block received their tray, the remaining tray will be passed out evenly to your people.

At this time, I'm handing every blood in the cell block, other tray. After, mop the floor, and wipe down the tables the same way you would wipe fingers prints off a gun.

Leaving food all over the table is the same as trashing someone hood.

You will have to answer to this.

Think, how can a card, chess, or dominoes game, be played on a nasty table.

Derek Grover

Don't just wipe shit on the floor
and go clean the fuckin shower.

Do everything right.

For this you will receive a welfare
pack.

A welfare pack is two envelopes,
one small bar of soap, and a golf
pencil, the pencil will be your shank.

You will be needing three of them.
Think, taking a chance with your life
for a welfare pack.

To get respect some niggas use
Blood and Cuz and some use pencil
lead. God has shown me that all you
will need is a powerful gimmick, all
you need is to give respect.

"God sent me here to tell you this
is my new journey. Unlike most I'm not
here for nothing."

The wheel was invented because man
couldn't hit shit throwing rocks and
the rock kept rolling after it missed
its target.

He did this in the rain and wondered why has mud formed a ring around the rock.

Maybe he saw a leaf blowing in the wind, still attached to the branch.

It keeps going in a circle, trying to break its own arm, only to fall to the ground as a propeller and die. The common man won't be going to jail or prison.

If everyone were common, there would be no Bible. My dream was to get my book into the prison system. God has shown and told me, "If you feel that way, D-Man, try it with your book of testimony."

We are creators here to follow the Creator. We create to become gods of what we create.

On my first day in the cell block, the Blood car surrounded me in my cell. As I looked over the tier, I knew the ground was 15 feet below me, and it was 21 feet to the top of my head.

Derek Grover

I made one request: "Just don't
disrespect my house, or I'm going to
throw you over the tier."

I was placed here by God to sit in
a cave with a rock blocking me in.

He's still trying to show me
something I can't find on the streets.
I saw the ground as a weapon,
calling out,

"Bring him to me, D-Man." Keep
in mind, Redrum is murder spelled
backwards.

Anyway, today a gangster from
Oceanside asked if he could move into
my cell. He was always fighting within
the Blood car.

For some reason, the Bloods hated
this nigga. He was constantly wiping
down the sink, scrubbing the toilet
after every use.

I told him, "I'm not with the
bullshit." He said he could fight and
knew MMA. I said, "Nigga, you can't
fight. Shut the fuck up. I'm not feeling
you. And fuck Oceanside." He just kept

wiping the toilet like it was a stolen gun with his prints on it.

In jail or prison, we call this hard time, and hard time comes with no skills. I threw his mattress over the tier. It hit the first tier floor below, right in front of the Black's shower, landing in a pool of shitty water.

The police came to my cell and asked me if I did that, pointing to the mattress.

The cell door slammed shut behind me, punctuating my defiant "yes." They took a report, documented the incident whatever. Later that day, Business, a gangster representing the Brims hardcore, strolled in, proudly proclaiming, "Yes, I'm with the business!"

"This cell needs a Blood in here, OG," he declared, using the term for an older, respected gangster.

"Alright," I said, keeping it simple.

He turned to Redrum, another Blood, and barked, "Yo, Blood, put all my shit on the top bunk." This was their loyalty dance, Redrum proving he'd bleed for the Blood car. Me? I barely blinked.

In the cage, power's a fickle thing. You can give it away and take it back all in the same day. Threats fly like pigeons here "I'll throw you over the tier!"

"You're dead!" but if someone keeps bugging you after that, it means one thing: they don't care, and willing to die for this shit.

Like Business, who one day sauntered up and asked, "Mind if I try on your glasses, D-Man?"

"Sure, go for it," I mumbled, not really caring either way.

He snatched the glasses, holding them precariously close to his face. "Damn, D-Man! I can see like a motherfucker with these on!"

His voice boomed with childlike wonder.

"Yeah, I can finally read that shit on the wall," he chuckled, referring to the prison rules and regulations plastered there. "Couldn't make out a word before."

"I got shot in the head at the taco shop on 43rd, in your hood," I offered, a touch of amusement in my voice. "A gangster unloaded a full clip on me while I was just chillin' in my car.

Blurred my vision something fierce, but hey, at least I see better now, right?"

He ignored my comment, completely absorbed in his newfound clarity.

He kept the glasses on, peering through the glass window on our cell door, even stretching his beard into a point for a closer look.

A sudden drumming sound reached my ears. Raindrops, I thought, picturing them hitting our small window at the back of the cell.

"D-Man, that ain't rain," Business scoffed. Just the sprinklers. I said, "hittin' the second tier windows."

I couldn't help but smirk. All this newfound vision, and he couldn't even tell the difference between rain and sprinklers.

He let out a short laugh, but the tension in his body remained.

All those push-ups he'd been doing all day hadn't calmed him down one bit.

I also noticed the Southsider's are doing the same thing. I saw them reading a copy of "ONEIGHTYSEVEN," in cell 187.

Chapter 3

GET THE FUCK OUT

The tension in the cell block was thick enough to cut with a shiv. Business and Redrum, our resident Bloods, were pushing their line with the Crips. Redrum, especially, was a walking provocation.

Every day, he'd taunt them, spitting out venom like, "fuck your dead homie! Paid his debt in full!" after a fight between rival gangster. Then came the cell brawl a bloody mess involving sworn enemies. Redrum sauntered back to our cell, a defiant glint in his eyes, followed by a pack of at least nine battle-hardened Crips.

He looked in my eyes, "I thought this nigga is going to kill one of your homeboys for that." He was referencing cell 130 the heart of 30th Street Crip territory. Yet, Redrum walked right past, unfazed. Remember, things are twisted here. Backwards, even. The deputies arrived, unlocked my cell, and delivered the message to Redrum:

"This ain't your cell. Get the fuck out." And get out he did.

Business, the dude they called Spoony back in the '80s, chuckled. "Yo, heard stories about a gangster named Spoony when I was a kid." "Been around that long, huh?" I replied, a hint of pride in my voice.

"Yeah, man," he continued, taking a break from his push-ups. "Grew up with the Bake Nuts myself. Craziest gang family in Southeast back in the day. Twenty-eight of them under one roof, if you can believe it."

He was perched backward on the toilet, meticulously breaking down a package of sausage to add to his Top ramen.

"Look, OG," he said, shaking his head, "you don't know how to stread."

He had a point. Spreads wasn't my forte. But something else caught my attention. "Funny you mention that," I started. "Turns out, your aunt was my homegirl back then. Me, her, and Capone used to run things way back when."

A flicker of surprise crossed Business' face.

"Damn, really? They went to prison, that's why the whole thing stopped. But you kept with it, huh?"

"Yeah, kept at it," I confirmed. "Even saw your aunt knock a nigga's tooth out once."

That's when I learned my lesson about underestimating women. My homegirl beat the living daylights out of a nigga faster than a speed bag.

From then on, I always kept my gun close, where I could to it fast, ready for anything.

The last time I saw her, we were counting our spoils in Tray Eight's bathroom eighty-eight bucks in food stamps we jacked from a crack house. She sat on the toilet, unlike Business here with his backward throne act.

She looked like a seasoned dice player, counting the loot, her voice calling out, "Spoony, Spoony, Spoony" faster than a gambling chant.

I swear, with the way she was spitting, I could have sold my gun and just bought some... well, you get the picture.

But I didn't sell the gun, and she didn't sell no pussy. That's why she's in prison with Capone, paying the price for that dope house robbery. Me? I'm still out here hustling, albeit with a bigger gun now. Chaos. We bolted out of the crack house, me through the back door, her with the cash.

I yelled at Capone, "Don't get caught with that bitch!" She had the loot, and him running with her to my car was a dead giveaway.

The police saw him sprint out the front, making him the clear suspect.

Who knew what he was thinking? He didn't even touch drugs, but that mistake cost him 25 years to life.

Street smarts say the police avoid shootouts by making you flee out the back. They knew I was involved but couldn't place me with her. A few hours later, back in the cell, Business said having a Blood in here was a good move. "More freedom to talk gang shit, I think."

But the Oceanside Blood they brought in wasn't the answer.

It wasn't the same. I tried pulling him aside, spitting some game, but he wasn't interested. All he craved was "cell block smoke" trouble brewing right here in our concrete cage.

The new Blood from Oceanside turned hostile real fast. He'd slam the air vent shut, then reopen it for no reason, all while giving us the silent treatment. When I called him out on his erratic behavior, he just shrugged it off like he didn't care, acting tough.

This dude was a walking contradiction all defiance with zero respect for either me or Business.

"Listen, homie," I growled, "I'm gonna block that damn vent myself, and you better leave it alone."

That didn't fly with him. He tensed up, ready for a fight. I stood my ground, right in his face.

But instead of swinging, he just backed into a corner, eyes wide.

"Yeah," I pressed, "that's what I thought. Now get the hell out of this cell."

There was no way I was sharing my space with this unpredictable nigga. "Look, homie," I continued, voice low but firm, "if things go south between us, every nigga in this cell block better make sure I walk out on top.

Fuck Oceanside this is San Diego, and in here, the San Diego car run things like a cartel."

With that, homie got the message respect was non-negotiable.

Oceanside? More like nowhere side. After tossing his entire collection onto the tier, the cops were back at my cell door.

Apparently, the new Blood thought a little begging could change my mind. Wrong place, wrong time. Here, decisions stick.

It started with the mattress. In one swift motion, I ripped it off his bunk and launched it out the cell door, landing in a crumpled heap on the stairs, sheets and yesterday's new blankets still clinging on. The rest of his belongings followed in a brutal eviction.

The police reappeared, this time taking a report and noting down the gang members who had barged into my cell, pleading for me to cut the new gangster some slack.

My actions, however, didn't sit
well with Bear, the Crips' shot caller
basically the all-knowing oracle on
top of the prison mountain.

And me? I felt like King Leonidas
in the movie "300," forced to answer
to this local authority for my
actions.

Anyway, Bear sent three Crips one
from the coast, two from his hood to
get me.

I knew they would be coming, just
like the police when they come to get
you. The only difference was, I wasn't
in handcuffs as they led me to the
first tier.

As I walked down the stairs, every
Crip in the cell block stood at their
window slots, watching. From cell 125
to 150, their eyes were on me.

The mattress I had thrown off the
tier the day before was still lying
on the ground in front of Bear's cell,
which was boarded up with cardboard
over the slot so no one could see
inside.

But you could tell he was fighting something.

I knocked on his cell door window with the back of my trigger finger. He tore the cardboard down from the top.

I couldn't see him clearly, but I didn't care.

Bear was fighting a murder beef and was losing. He was locked in like the Beast from the movie Glass.

Despite the lack of a firearm, I couldn't shake the image of him losing a fight in that cell if he had a knife. I pressed my ear against the cold metal door frame, catching his muffled voice.

"D-Man, what the fuck, cuz? You aired the whole Crip car out like dirty laundry!" His voice boomed, laced with fury.

"Yo fuckin ass better never pull that stunt again. I don't want the Southsiders to see that shit, you feel me?"

A heavy silence followed, broken
only by his final words, delivered
in a low growl. "RIP to your dead
homeboys, cuz."

I met his single, rage-filled yellow
eye through the remaining cardboard
and spoke. On the under the homeboys
call me, "ONEIGHTYSEVEN.

At this point, I have a confusing
look on my face. My AK-47 is in the
trunk of my car. And my car is still
sitting in the San Diego Police
impound yard. But I still know, that
shit don't mean nothing in here.

I would like you to also know, this
place is not the streets. To tell you
the truth, Its, not going to be.

If anyone ask you to do something with
respect, in here you better do it.

In the cell block, the demographics
painted a vivid picture: 36 Crips,
20 Southsider Hispanics, 10 Lakeside
Mafia, and 13 Bloods from various
factions like Skyline, Lincoln, the
Brims, and Fruit Town, Compton.

Despite the numbers, Bear remained elusive, confined within the confines of his cell.

Instead, he operated through a runner, a gangster without a specific affiliation but facing the same life sentence as everyone else.

This runner navigated the intricate politics of the cell block, ensuring Bear's influence extended beyond his physical presence.

This runner's notoriety preceded him; he had attempted to take out the police at the 62nd Encanto trolley stop, cementing his reputation within the cell block.

Chapter 4

I'M DOWN FOR YOU

Awaken by a 4:00 am wake-up call, court day demanded an early start. First in line for breakfast, we devoured a rare, hearty meal of eggs, hash browns, bread, and milk filling sensation almost foreign in this concrete jungle.

Sleep hadn't touched me the night before, but then again, it rarely did.

Fifty of us, inmates from cell blocks A and B, shuffled through the main block tunnel, flanked by a sheriff's escort. The full moon cast an eerie glow on the caged-in walkway leading to the transfer department.

The air hung crisp and cold.

This day marked my first meeting with my lawyer, Doug Miller. Polished and professional, he exuded an aura of competence.

He took a genuine interest in my case, assuring me we had a fighting chance but only at trial.

The downside? The D.A. was gunning for 25 years to life. His sharp features and confident demeanor brought to mind Perry Mason himself, the legendary lawyer from the TV show.

I told him I hope he is a fighter because I was. He had a copy of ONEIGHTYSEVEN, in his hand. He said, "D-Man I'm down for you, I will do my best to get you off of these false charges. I can see they're out to get you."

"I'll see you at your Prelim, on January 1."

I said, "I'm cool with that too." Later sitting in the transfer tank, a gangster came up to me and said, "O.G. did you write the book, ONEIGHTYSEVEN?

Remember me I played Pop Warner with your son?

Hunter the quarterback. He said, that's me.

You gave me a book when I was a kid. I remember. What happened to you? Lincoln, OG, you know what's up.

I got caught on a hot one.

What they hit you with? 26 years with a "L." The "L" means life.

The next time I saw him, was in the court tanks, fighting, with fellow gang members. I stood over him and said, "fuck that nigga, fuck that slob up."

He stopped. Later he told me he heard someone say slob nigga, it made him think. "Who is that."

God stopped the fight in a strange way, but it worked.

Today at the General's table, the Bloods' presence had dwindled to just three gangsters: Business, Fruit Town, and Redrum.

I brought it to Business attention. He said, "The last 300." I said, "yeah, like King Leonidas and his last two general." "You won't get stab by the spears, but all the arrows are pointed at you."

Fruit Town understood now that I was all in too.

Later, a slight knock at my cell door signaled Fruit Town's arrival, bringing more drama from the Blood car.

He began, "Look here, O.G. niggas, we're fighting in the court tank.

They heard you say 'get that slob.' Is it true?"

"Yes," I said.

"Let me put you up."

The Bloods kept yammering in my ear all day with their blood talk. I stayed silent to keep the peace, but in my mind, I was thinking, "Fuck these slobs."

When they started fighting each other, my thoughts slipped out. The Bloods were banging on everyone, which led to so many fights. They were brawling in front of the Crips, Whites, and Southsiders.

I couldn't intervene because I'm a Crip. But when I said "slob," it made them stop and think.

I thanked God for that. I told Fruit Town to go back and tell them what I said.

"I wanted to tell you, but the court run made me tired," I explained, still lying on my bunk.

Court runs are stressful.

I was offered a 25-year plea bargain.

The next morning, I went to the chapel and asked every Black, White, and Mexican inmate to pray for the Trolley Cop Killer.

The young inmate, facing 89 years to life, showed me a picture of his son before I went to sleep. His son's image haunted my dreams, particularly his fingers, as if they were throwing up the 40s, representing Bear's hood.

In my mind, I couldn't shake the thought of "Lil Bear" and "Baby Bear."

The atmosphere in the cell block was tense, especially among the Southsiders and Surenos, who appeared militant.

As I walked past each cell, I noticed them engaging in rigorous exercises—lifting water bags, doing push-ups, and burpees.

It seemed like they were preparing for something, but it was hard to discern as they kept themselves rolled up, remaining guarded.

Their behavior indicated a readiness for action. They never fully unpacked their belongings when entering the cell block, reserving that only for solitary confinement.

Even when lying down with their mattresses rolled up for use as pillows, their eyes remained open, alert to any potential threat.

They always salute me.

Anyway, I do pushups in the morning and at night to make sure I keep it real.

Chapter 5

EVERY TIME HE EXHALED

I visited the jail chaplain, Mike, who shared a perspective on Jesus' crucifixion that left me stunned.

He explained that Jesus' feet were nailed to the cross at a 45-degree angle to bear the weight of his body.

The Romans did this to prevent him from locking his legs, adding further agony.

Mike described how the weight on Jesus' shoulders tore them out of their sockets, and made it hard, to breathe, Jesus had to push up on the nails in his feet with every exhale.

Reflecting on Jesus' words from the cross, "Father, forgive them, for they do not know what they do," I realized the depth of suffering he endured.

Mike's insights were eye-opening; I couldn't help but feel humbled by the revelation. It was a perspective I doubted I would have encountered had I not been in this place.

I knew I would find a better understanding of God. At this point of my work, I will start to tell you how I see the presence of God.

Chaplin Mike said, "God says meter will fall to the earth like figs from a fig tree."

For the blood and the crips, It, gets more dangerous. This morning a blood gangster told another crip, fuck your dead homeboy. Like every one before him he went into cell 132 and came out puffed up like it wasn't shit.

Hand over his left eye. He just walked the cell block floor like he was on the streets. I think if he was on the streets he would have come back with a gun to shoot and killed everybody.

Business walks the cell block with no socks.

The situation is part of gangbanging. Everyone staring at me, I think they think I might be the next shot caller, If I do it would be the San Diego car. Blacks, are powerful in here.

It gets more dangerous every day. Some inmates are out to court. When they come back, they will be lifers.

A new bunch of gangsters will be ready to put it down. I'm doing more pushups.

Gangsters are screaming out what set they clam.

As some inmates departed for court, their return as lifers loomed ominously. Their absence would create a void, soon to be filled by a fresh wave of gangsters eager to assert their dominance.

In preparation for the escalating tensions, I dedicated myself to rigorous workouts, bracing for the inevitable clashes and ensuring my readiness for whatever may come.

Meanwhile, gangsters continued to proclaim their allegiance, their voices echoing the volatile atmosphere of the cell block.

Today promises to be anything but smooth sailing.

From dawn till dusk, it's been a relentless barrage of fists meeting flesh, violence lurking just beyond the peripheral vision of the entire cell block.

To glance in the direction of an ongoing assault is to invite blame upon oneself, a costly mistake that carries dire consequences.

Each morning, as cell doors swing open, Bloods and Crips alike embark on a solemn pilgrimage to cell 130 on the first tier, a rendezvous point for countless gang skirmishes.

The frequency of these clashes is such that inmates resort to growing beards as a feeble attempt to conceal the harsh reality of life behind bars.

One gangster stepped in the cell.

His heart went down to his feet and into his socks, where you slip and slide if you don't take them off.

Besides its impossible for a blood to win if they're 30 crips standing over you.

It won't work that way. When the crip came out his cell, he looked like he took a shower and was putting on sports deodorant.

"I'm 12 and 2, cuz," he declared, his words echoing with a weight that reverberated through the gathered Southsiders, despite the familiar cadence of his proclamation.

For my endeavors today, my cell door will remain ajar, granting me the freedom to move about as I please. Yet, even as this gesture of trust is extended, Bear looms at my cell door, a harbinger of ominous tidings.

"Triple OG," he intones, his voice weighted with the gravity of his confession, "I got found guilty for a hot one. It's time to clean house."

A "hot one" signifies a murder, and "cleaning house" entails exacting vengeance upon anyone who dares to encroach upon one's personal boundaries, be it within the confines of jail or prison. It's a stark reminder of the ruthless politics that govern gang life.

In Bear's words lies an implicit warning: "I eliminate gangsters, D-Man. The primal instinct within me compels me to assert my dominance and protect my territory."

"I feel like God put me here to help you," I confessed to him, the weight of my words resonating within the confines of my cell.

The moniker "G-block" has become a familiar refrain among both the Bloods and the Crips, a testament to the emerging role I seem to be playing in this volatile environment.

Derek Grover

From the first tier, Chill Dogg's voice carries throughout the day and even infiltrates my dreams, a constant presence that disrupts my sleep.

He converses with the thirty Crips stationed outside his cell, their discussions punctuating the silence of the night.

When the chatter ceases, I awaken abruptly, only to find Fruit Town inspecting my shank with keen interest.

"Hey, what's up, Gee? If you need it, it's yours," I offer casually, confident in my ability to fashion another one if necessary.

"I have a feeling you're going to need it," I add cryptically.

Rumors of an impending "house cleaning" circulate, signaling a turbulent day ahead.

Fruit Town, a newcomer to the prison system, may not fully comprehend the dynamics at play, particularly the deep-seated animosity

52

between San Diego and Los Angeles gang members.

Positioned at the center of the cell block, I command a visible presence, a silent assertion of power that resonates with the control tower looming in front of my cell.

Adjacent to the showers designated for the Whites and Southsiders, a protocol unfolds when they choose to bathe, entering the shower area in groups of four for added security.

Introducing himself as B.K. Butler, he adopted a street moniker that hinted at a darker persona.

"Like in blood killer Butler," I remarked, to which he responded with a grim acknowledgment. Reflecting on the significance of names, I couldn't help but draw parallels to the power they held in shaping one's identity. He looks like Bluto from the cartoon Popeye the Sailor. Butler maintained a somber demeanor reminiscent of his expression during my testimony in the chapel.

With a grim smile etched on his face, Butler revealed his ailment.

"I'm sick, D-Man. What do you have for my spread?" he inquired, prompting me to offer him a pack of fiery hot beef jerky.

As I reclined on my bunk afterward, the intense heat of the jerky triggered an uncomfortable sensation, causing the saliva in my throat to backwash into my nose, resulting in a burning sensation akin to smoke billowing from a bull's nostrils.

The packaging boasted, "Feel good about feeding your hunger while you feed your wild side," a slogan that offered little comfort as I endured the lingering burn throughout the night, forcing me to remain upright for hours.

This isn't a tale—it's the unvarnished truth.

The following day, I perused the packaging once more. A Somalian gangster caught sight of me shirtless and remarked, "Damn, D-Man, your ass is big."

I quipped back, "I always keep my guns hidden," eliciting a chuckle from him. Comparing myself to Jack Wilson from the film Shane, I emphasized my prowess as a gunslinger, boasting of my stature and the metaphorical "guns" I carried.

"Now you can see what I'm made of," I declared, to which he simply shrugged and walked away.

In Shane, the titular character famously said, "Some gunslingers use two guns, but one is all you need."

A curious observation: Redrum's lyrical abilities seem to peak when his eyes are swollen shut.

"D-Man, stay up, baby. God just gave me a vision—you're gonna make it big," Dookie Stick exclaimed, his voice filled with conviction. "When you get out, tell all the youngsters the truth. They'll listen to you.

You're old school bringing it to the new school."

As he spoke, I couldn't help but feel a sense of affirmation.

"I saw you walk by; God told me to tell you this," he continued.

"I know," I replied, recognizing the divine guidance that had brought me to this moment.

"He told me, too. He said you're here for a reason—to free us from the grip of our foul deeds."

"Dookie Stick, you're strong," I remarked, admiring his resilience. "You look like you could roll a nigga up and flush him down the toilet like a piece of toilet tissue." I paused before adding, "If I had one bitch in here with 50 niggas, I would share her with everyone.

On my last day out, I would have 50 niggas at my funeral."

He stopped me as I walked the cell block, and in that moment, I felt the undeniable presence of God in everything I did.

Memories of God's visitation in my cell at San Quentin flooded my mind, reminding me of the divine purpose guiding my journey.

Chapter 6

TURN IN YOUR RAZOR

In the wee hours of the morning, Chill Dogg sent Blue Light with a grim update: the cops had nabbed my homeboy yesterday. Caught him puffing on a cigarette in front of his grandma's place.

Poor guy tried to bolt inside, but they zapped him with a taser. It's a scenario I try not to dwell on. My crew always seems to forget, but I never do: I'm the one who always ends up in cuffs just for being around them.

They always reassure me, saying, "D-Man, they're not gonna bust you for that," but they're always wrong.

At 3:00 AM, The Trolley Cop Killer stares at me, his gaze piercing through the dimness, from under his blanket.

He looks like a specter, black and ominous, with those tiny, black eyes fixated on me.

Wrapped in a white sheet, he resembles the Mummy Man, a reminder of the day I caught a bullet in my head while sitting in my car.

All because of that. I don't fuck around. As soon as I got off my bunk, I made it clear to him that I was back on my feet. "What time is it?" he asked. "Sorry, can't tell. I don't have my glasses," I replied, sensing his stare. I had to meet his eyes head-on, ready for whatever was coming.

"Does it matter? I'll get with you," I snapped, gearing up for a potential confrontation.

The next day, my attorney visited me in jail. He just received the police report and needed time to go through it.

"Give me 45 days," he requested.

Forty-five days later, in court, he dropped a bombshell: "They're trying to throw you in for 25 years to life."

But just as I was processing this, a court deputy interrupted, "Let's go, Grover, you're out of here."

I relayed the news to my folks, resigned to my fate.

Hoping for a swift transfer back to George Baily Detention Facility, I was pulled back into court by my attorney.

"Derek, I misspoke earlier. I told your people you were facing 25 to life by mistake. Don't worry, you'll be fine," he reassured me.

I trusted him. His law partner kept reassuring me, saying, "He likes you, Derek. He's going to fight for you." The next morning, while taking my morning piss, I glanced out my cell door and saw two new Crip gang members entering the cell block.

The Southsiders never fret about clashing with the Crips or Bloods, whether in jail or prison.

Along with the newcomers, two more Crips joined our ranks. It was our usual daily lockup, and we'd be released to roam the cell block in about four hours.

During those hours, Trolley Cop Killer spent his time regaling me with tales of his foolishness in his final moments of freedom.

He recounted how Business had swindled everyone in a dice game the night before, which didn't sit well with the Crips.

They were ready to retaliate until lockdown was called.

The next morning, I admonished him, "Don't do that again," before walking away. Hours later, as I strolled the cell block, he approached me, asking, "Spoony, why did you say that?" I replied, "You took food out of the Crips' mouths. You need to think.

I give the Bloods three trays of hash browns and eggs every day each. That's real. Don't do anything to draw the wrath of the Crip car."

We walked halfway around, then headed to the Whites' side of the cell block, leaning against the wall. The Whites approached us, asking, "D-Man, are you coming to the service today?" I affirmed, "Yeah."

Turning to Business, I suggested we keep moving, so we proceeded to the black section of the cell block, again resting our backs against the wall.

No White inmates ever ventured into this area. I informed Business that I was going to talk to the new inmate and headed towards his cell. At this point, Business understood that I was fully committed.

I ascended the stairs to reach cell 233 where the new gangster resided. Though he couldn't see me, he sensed my presence. Positioned at the end of the second tier, he had the last cell.

"Hey, I'm D-Man Bloccide Crip," I introduced myself.

"I'm Skeet, Skyline," he replied, indicating his affiliation with Skyline but his non-active status.

Listening closely to his words, I gauged his gang involvement.

"Did you come down from the pen?" I inquired.

"Yeah, but the Feds," he responded, revealing a 14-year stint but also indicating a pending case in the State.

You'll be going home soon, I reassured him. "Would you like a care package to keep up your size?"

I sent him a package containing soup, fruit punch, pretzels, M&Ms, and an apple. He expressed gratitude. Later, I briefed him on the cell block's politics. Introduce yourself whenever you're ready, I prompted.

He headed to the shower, rolling up his pants legs and removing his shirt to shave his head.

As he did, I couldn't help but notice the multitude of cuts on his

Derek Grover

back, more than Interstate 8 has
passing through various cities towards
Blackwater military base in Campo,
California.

With his pants legs cuffed to
prevent them from getting wet, he
positioned himself in front of the
mirror, resembling the action figure
HeeMan. "Skeet, everyone's sneaking
glances at you," I remarked.

Ignoring the guard's instruction
to turn in his razor, he defiantly
declared, "D-Man, screw that."
Consequently, they cut off the TV.
Unfazed, he continued shaving his
face, skillfully grooming his goatee,
albeit at the expense of everyone
missing the last fifteen minutes of
Monday Night Football.

He strolled past the white's tables,
prompting them to rise and silently
scrutinize the cuts on his back,
exchanging glances but saying nothing.

From the second tier, I whistled
down to Joker, the white shot caller,
and chuckled. "I'll handle it," I
assured him, and indeed I did.

"Skeet, man, that was hilarious,"
I told him. The following day, he
took on the role of a worker, even
offering me extra trays. It was just
the two of us at the bloods' generals
table, surrounded by stacked trays of
buttery hot french toast and orange
juice. Meanwhile, the Southsiders were
enduring numerous beatdowns.

From the tower, the police ordered,
"Everyone move from in front of cell
220 now," marking the beginning of a
celebration with glasses of Promo. The
cell block was bustling with activity.

The Trolley Cop Killer was refusing
to eat any jail house food It's the
same routine at breakfast every day
if it's not hard-boiled eggs, he won't
touch it.

He'll push his tray to the center
of the table, convinced that's how it's
done, oblivious to the fact that this
will be his reality for the rest of
his life.

The truth is, he's unknowingly
draining his family's resources. You
might wonder how, who's footing the

bill for the peanut butter and jelly sandwiches?

Oh, and showers? Forget about it.

He settles for a bird bath in the sink, a habit he picked up from his days of homelessness before his crime spree.

That's how I know he's not a true gangster. But he's young, he'll learn, though likely the hard way. I dread having to document more about him because it won't paint a pretty picture.

San Francisco's Disco, as he likes to call himself, was partying it up at the Pyramid on MiraMar Road in San Diego when the police put an end to his fun.

He found himself behind bars after kicking out the window of a police cruiser, inadvertently injuring an officer below the eye with a piece of broken glass.

That act landed him a six-month sentence, swiftly transforming him from a three-time wrestling champion at the University of Nebraska to just another inmate overnight.

This guy is as square as they come if he tried to rob you, you could probably talk him out of it.

He'll point a gun at your head, and all you'd need to say is, "You look like my brother," and he'd shift it to your neck. Protest, and he'd aim lower.

Try another excuse, and he'd likely drop the weapon and bolt.

But despite his lack of street smarts, he's good for one thing being unaffiliated.

He's inadvertently helping me refine my communication skills, which is why you won't find the word "nigga" on this page of the book.

He might just be a divine messenger, sent by God to teach me how to carry myself better.

He's the only one who's ever had the guts to tell me when my words stink, and strangely enough, I appreciate it.

Plus, he's a pro at putting people in their place, and I'm okay with that too sometimes we need a good shake-up.

He's also got a knack for appreciating my street jokes about women and criminals.

Fridays are particularly tense around here, especially with a lot of inmates returning to the cell block in green jumpsuits, freshly sentenced, too life.

Chapter 7

38 YEARS TO LIFE

In these parts, the green jumpsuits signify lifers. Take JB, a Linda Vista Asin Crips gangster. I crossed paths with him about a week ago, and he approached me, asking if I'd written a book.

"Yeah, that's right, homie," I confirmed. But then I asked, "What's the catch?" You got some pork skins to sell? I had some skins, but I couldn't sell him any I liked them too much.

Instead, I offered him half the bag. He headed to my cell to pick them up, and when I poured some into my palm and handed him the bag, he seemed perplexed, like he didn't quite know what to do with it.

Later that week, he returned from court wearing the green jumpsuit.

I observed his actions closely.

He made a call from the black's phone rack on the wall, and at the same time, the Crips approached the phone rack, standing over him, laughing and joking.

The gangster kept shifting the phone from ear to ear, covering the one not in use with his hand, while the Crips continued their banter in front of him.

Meanwhile, the Linda Vista Crip repeatedly hit the loud button on the phone, much like pressing a button on a street pole. Once he hung up, everyone dispersed.

Later, I learned that he'd been sentenced to 38 years to life for punching his homeboy in the face and taking his cell phone.

It made me contemplate offering him a full bag of hot pork skins as a gesture of goodwill.

So, I punctured a hole in the bag to let the air out and slid them under his cell door.

Baby Durk, from the coast, picked them up, consumed them, and expressed his gratitude, saying, "Thank you, G-Block." As his murder trial loomed for the following week, someone remarked, "Okay, but things won't be okay for long."

Bear's routine of brutalizing gangsters continued unabated.

At dinner, amidst the clatter of utensils, we suddenly heard the sickening sound of fists meeting flesh. Sensing trouble, I peered out from my cell door.

There, Bear emerged from his cell with an expression that seemed to say, "You can clean up now."

He prowled the cell block like Mike Tyson after a knockout in the ring.

Meanwhile, Skeet seemed displeased with the food, twirling his tray like a merry-go-round. "D-Man, you want this crap?" he asked.

I declined, mentioning I had plenty of canteen stashed away. Skeet dumped his milk on the tray and tossed it in the trash before hurrying back to his cell.

Later, he returned, reflecting on our earlier conversation about the phone. I offered him my phone code so he could reach the streets, especially since he was upset his own wasn't working.

Unfortunately, it was too late; we had to lock up until the next day.

After spending 14 years behind bars, it's easy to feel like you've become just another number, lost in the system.

During one quiet moment, the Trolley Cop Killer accused me of being heartless. I countered, telling him I knew wasn't a real gangster, he couldn't take his eyes off me and that he was likely putting on a front.

But he remained silent, perhaps too young to fully understand. His gaze seemed to ask, "How do I escape this shit, D-Man?"

I urged him to develop his skills to navigate through.

Meanwhile, the crips were refusing to lock down, signaling potential trouble ahead.

Perhaps it was because I was sitting in the front row, paying close attention, or maybe not. The prison chaplain's words seemed to pierce through the tension of our situation.

He reassured us that God had a plan for each of us, urging us not to feel distraught. While I could accept his message, I doubted whether others shared my sentiments.

After all, I could write in here but not on the streets.

Despite the challenges, I found myself treated like a five-star general.

More and more gang members and criminals were opening up to me about their cases, all of which were high-profile crimes in the city and county of San Diego.

The previous night, I even shared jokes with the police, finding some solace in moments of unexpected camaraderie.

"Why do you leave your gun outside?" I asked. His response was simple: "That's how we do it."

He went on to mention having a Mac-90 in the trunk of his car, casually parked in the lot. I couldn't help but feel like Will Smith in the movie Hancock, who could have easily broken out, just to get to the Mac-90 but chose not to.

Eventually, they let him out to fight crime, but he seemed unfazed by it all.

"Fuck it, let the police try it," he shrugged. Meanwhile, the Southsiders' shot caller was heading to prison that day.

As he paced up and down the tier, the sliding sound of his slip-ons woke me up. His name was Misery.

Two hours later, we were released into the cell block, where a new Southsider shot caller took charge.

He was a fat Sureno who didn't quite fit the image. However, his size made it clear: don't pick a fight with him in the cell, or he'd likely overpower you. As he stood in line to collect food trays from a black gangster, the dynamics of power in the cell block shifted once again.

He tried to collect his cellmates tray.

But was told no by a black gangster handing out tray. The black gangster said, your cellmate will have to come get his own tray.

The shot caller had no less then 10 Southsider gang members with him. The line was jammed up. The Sureno said, give me the tray that's how we do it on our tier.

The Sureno insisted, "Yeah, right," and this sparked Fruit Town's attention. He commanded, "Give him the trays, BLOOD," but the gangster stood firm.

Despite the collective chorus urging him to relent, he continued to refuse.

Fruit Town's frustration boiled over as he clenched his fist on the table and declared, "Let's go to your cell."

The gangster, still wearing plastic food serving gloves, reluctantly agreed.

In a flash, Fruit Town leaped from the table and made his way to the gangster's cell, his focus narrowed like tunnel vision.

I turned to Business and instructed, "Go get that nigga.

But Business hesitated, looking at me as if to say, "You go get that nigga."

Chapter 8

THE STORM IS BREWING

Later that day, Fruit Town mentioned he tried counting to ten to calm himself down.

I'm relieved he took a moment because this guy is massive, a former San Diego State football player serving time for a bank takeover robbery.

Today has arrived, but last night brought even more tension to the cell block.

While I was at chapel, the crip car was up to its usual business. Blood Killer stopped by my cell and delivered a grave message: "D-Man, you should know, shit's about to hit the fan."

He explained that Dookie Stick had taken it upon himself to declare as the shot caller for the blacks, even though the black population is predominantly made up of crips.

Naturally, this didn't sit well with the crips. Pookie mentioned he was ready for seven-on-one fades.

The weight of responsibility.

It was the same Pookie who took on the gangster from Lincoln. Blood Killer's inquiry seemed to imply he valued my 27 years of experience in this life.

"Good looking out," I responded, relieved that the burden didn't fall on my shoulders. "Fifty crips is a big cake to swallow," I remarked. "Stay up, O.G.," Blood Killer said before departing with Dookie Stick.

Later, Dookie Stick returned to offer his perspective.

"G-Block, you good?" he asked. "No doubt, my nigga, what's up?" I replied.

He confided that things were looking grim for him, mentioning his fighting prowess. "Dookie Stick, you need to un-ball your fists and put your socks back on," I advised.

"These niggas will wrap you up with one on your legs, one on your chest, and one on your neck, while everyone else beats your face."

I urged him, "Go ask them for forgiveness."

Grateful, he acknowledged, "Thank you, OG. You're the only one to tell me this." I replied, "Walk away and do the right thing.

I'm heading back to my bunk." Adding, "You don't want to wake up with this shit in the morning; it's human nature."

The next day, we were served two hard-boiled eggs and two hash browns for breakfast, a good day to pick up where we left off.

Suddenly, the lock-down alarm pierced through my sleep, making me think it was chow time and that I had overslept.

In the commotion, I heard Dookie Stick shout, "Nigga, I'll beat that ass, cuz," and for a moment, I thought he was referring to a game of chess.

But then, the police began yelling "lock it down" over the loudspeaker, echoing like the voice of the Wizard in the movie "Wizard of Oz."

Peering out of my cell door, I spotted Dookie Stick heading back to his cell.

After exchanging RIPs, to all the crips he retreated into his cell with his fist balled up and shut the door behind him. The sound of Deputy Douglas's footsteps approached, and soon he was being led away in cuffs, the metallic clink, clink, clinks echoing throughout the cell block.

Meanwhile, tensions simmered as a gang member called out the Trolley Cop Killer for his purported lack of authenticity.

The impending confrontation was
slated to unfold in cell 131. But
before delving into that, I had a
visit to the prison doctor scheduled
for today.

I sought medical attention due to
a chronic dry eye that often felt
as if a piece of glass were lodged
within it.

The doctor, a woman, administered
gel into my eye and dimmed the lights,
utilizing a blue light to detect any
foreign objects.

I recounted an incident from a few
years ago when a piece of glass had
indeed become embedded in my eye from
a broken car window I used in a crime.

After her examination, she
reassured me that there was nothing
present, emphasizing that if there
were, my tears would naturally flush
it out. Nonetheless, she explained
how the gel might create a sensation
akin to having something lodged within
the eye.

She mentioned that in my case,
tears might flow backward, prompting me

to inquire why I found myself shedding tears every night over my deceased homeboys.

Her response was simple: "That's probably it." Despite her age, she exuded a pleasant scent and chewed gum as she stood close to me.

Being a handsome man, I could tell she enjoyed my company just as much as I appreciated hers.

Upon returning to the cell block, I shared with everyone that I wasn't fixated on the female doctor, yet her demeanor felt reminiscent of someone braiding my hair in my youth.

Her special attention left me feeling good all over.

More so, I was relieved to learn that my nightly tears weren't solely about my lost homeboys, as I had assumed.

In jail, finding positivity in every situation becomes crucial.

As it's nearing 7:00 p.m., the fight will commence once the first tier is released from lockdown.

I hope my cellmate emerges victorious against this gangster. During dinner, I slipped the gangster that The Trolley Cop Killer was set to fight an extra hamburger, hoping it would slow him down.

Let's see if it works. With the day's drama behind us, it's now 9:50 p.m. and we're locked in our cells for the night.

The Trolley Cop Killer made his way to cell 131 and initiated the altercation swiftly.

He let the other gangster enter the cell first, then rushed in himself, delivering rapid and effective punches.

The opposing gangster, unaccustomed to cell fights and still wearing his socks, was clearly outmatched.

In such fights, it's crucial not to risk injuring your hands by hitting the wall or bunks, throwing punches incorrectly.

I advised The Trolley Cop Killer to
lift his opponent onto the table to
keep him off his feet, avoid lowering
his head, and pull him into his
punches by grabbing his shirt.

I emphasized the importance of
persistence, as nobody would intervene
to stop the fight.

The goal was to make the opponent
tap out, and I even suggested
resorting to biting if necessary, as
bite marks leave a lasting impression.

The following day, The Trolley Cop
Killer accompanied me to the chapel,
and as we walked in, we were greeted
with expressions of "praise the Lord"
from everyone who saw us.

Despite being in a fight, I had been
praying for The Trolley Cop Killer,
hoping he would choose good over evil.

To my relief, he made the right
choice, and the altercation ended
fairly, without any gang intervention.

Later, the police surprised us
with a new 32-inch flat-screen TV, a

significant upgrade from our previous 19-inch set.

It was a Christmas gift that lifted everyone's spirits.

I also received a visit from a chaplain from the streets, a professional interaction that felt like a blessing from God.

Initially, I couldn't help but ask repeatedly if he was the police, as his suit gave off a law enforcement vibe.

However, he reassured me, revealing his true identity as a plumber by trade, evident from the cuts on his hands.

Amidst the chaos, with violence escalating, the presence of 30 deputies entering the cell block signaled a much-needed break.

They instructed us to strip off our clothing and lined us up against the wall, bringing a sense of order to the tumultuous environment.

The deputies entered with large trash bins and instructed us to deposit our clothing into them.

As we complied, curiosity got the better of us, and we kept glancing back to see what they were removing from our cells.

However, the sergeant sternly commanded us to keep our focus on the wall.

Their warning was clear: if we continued to disobey and look around, they threatened to revoke the Christmas gift they had bestowed upon us just two days prior.

Chapter 9

FUCK YOU AND YOUR PEOPLE

The 32-inch flat screen emerged from the box, a welcome upgrade. After providing us with new clothes, they ushered us back to our cells, allowing us to keep what they had left behind.

Returning to inspect our reactions, the deputies engaged in laughter and banter with us. Despite the overall positive turn of events, uncertainty lingered about what tomorrow might bring.

Disco, hailing from the bay, suggested that both Trolley Cop Killer and I belong in jail.

Dismissing his comment, I retorted, "Fuck you and your people." He boasted, claiming he would run circles around us on the streets. I countered, asserting that I wouldn't hesitate to bust on anyone that dared to be a threat.

Determined to prove my point, I challenged him to get off his bunk, removing my socks to showcase my readiness.

I warned him against his smoker habit, emphasizing my reluctance to associate with such behavior even miles away on the streets.

While he resides in San Francisco, I reminded him that he better keep quiet. Just then, my name echoed through the loudspeaker, signaling a visit. Ignoring his presence, I challenged him to a fight before I left.

He remained silent as I headed for my visit. Upon reaching the crowded visiting room, I discovered that my visitor hadn't arrived, leaving me to wait it out with the others. Thirty minutes later, we were escorted back to the cell block.

At the black's phone, I removed my socks, preparing for potential confrontation as I returned to my cell.

Gripping the door handle, I braced myself for whatever awaited inside. Upon entering, I confronted him, ready for action. However, Disco seemed nonchalant, responding with a casual "nothing."

Asserting my readiness with my socks and glasses, I expressed my disappointment over the missed visit, my resolve unbroken. Turning my attention to the Chargers-Titans game playing outside my cell door, I remained focused on the match.

After the game, Disco approached me with a handshake, perhaps signaling a truce or a newfound respect. I extended my hand in apology, initiating a wave of laughter and banter that carried us through the night and into the morning.

The following day, amidst a sea of 45 inmates, we were the sole representatives of our race at breakfast.

After he finished eating, we returned to our cell, engaging in a discussion that delved into philosophical territory, where he emerged victorious, earning the respect of those who bore witness.

With tensions easing from the turmoil of previous days, yesterday marked the first chapel service since Christmas.

Unfortunately, many missed the holiday service due to the deputies' refusal to unlock our cells. This place operates like the Wizard of Oz— everything seemingly controlled by unseen hands, remote and computerized. While this may suit some, those seeking deeper peace find themselves unsettled by the impersonal mechanisms governing our lives.

Amidst the array of inmates, encompassing both gang members and criminals, a collective frustration brewed over the deputies' practice of preventing some from attending chapel services. I, too, harbored these sentiments but kept them to myself until today. Several inmates approached me, seeking assistance.

"OG, we've drafted a grievance complaint," they said. "We believe the guards are responsible for our inability to attend religious services."

Accepting the role of cell block ambassador, I took charge of the paperwork, crafting the complaint which the inmates then filed as a class action.

It was a task undertaken by battle-hardened individuals, many with a history of violence and crime.

Completing the paperwork, I felt a sense of fulfillment.

From nothing, something good had emerged. The essence of our complaint was encapsulated in the statement: "We, the inmates of cell block 6B, require a conducive environment to worship and seek forgiveness for our sins."

I added, "The deputy team has a reputation for toying with inmates, treating the intercom system like a hip-hop booth.

They scratch records to hip-hop beats and blast gangster rap."

Later, The Trolley Cop Killer informed me that Dookie Stix had been jumped.

Bear and T-Rex, the latter facing a murder charge linked to an incident outside Dr. J's liquor store involving Pookie and Boxhead, were responsible.

It was Bear's way of asserting dominance, sending a clear message that the San Diego crip car wouldn't be controlled by a gangster from Chicago.

I offered some sobering advice, telling him, "One day, your protection will vanish, and people will come after you relentlessly." His expression betrayed vulnerability, on the verge of tears. "See, I know you're not a true gangster."

Furthermore, I made it clear that when it came to Bear, I wouldn't confront him in his cell.

Instead, I planned to face him head-on in the center of the cell block.

To demonstrate what true fighting skills entail, both on the streets and in the confines of the cell block, I instructed, "Go tell him and see what the consequences will be."

Bear had a routine: he never emerged from his cell without first pumping himself up. He'd do countless pushups to bulk up, akin to a turkey flaunting its tail feathers. He preyed on new arrivals, exploiting their unfamiliarity with the harsh realities of prison life.

It was a harsh adjustment for those accustomed to having things their way on the streets.

Meanwhile, the Southern Mexican gang members were intoxicated on pruno, a potent prison wine. With tensions running high, everyone had to be on alert, as riots often erupted under such circumstances.

The drunken brawls echoed throughout the cell block, like feet in the bath tub.

Recall when I mentioned the table seating arrangement all the blacks occupied the left side of the arrow, with my seat positioned at the tip.

I see myself as the sharp tip of the arrow, always ready to cut through any situation. Just like how I use movie references like comparing the voices from the control booth to the Wizard of Oz or likening myself to Denzel Washington in Man on Fire to describe what's happening around me.

If anyone decides to mess with me, I'll channel Denzel's intensity from that film, making it clear that I don't tolerate any nonsense, especially not from the Southern Mexican gang members who are well aware of my reputation.

At 2:00 a.m., the cell block goes into its nightly lockdown routine. During the count, one of the deputies notices that a gangster's face looked like it had been through a meat grinder.

Chapter 10

DRUNK OFF PRUNO

During count, you've got to stand up to show the deputies you're in general good health. But sometimes, it's not just your typical head count it's more like a meat grinder, with fists and feet flying everywhere.

One inmate ended up looking like he'd been through a meat grinder himself. They called him to the box, popped his cell door, and sat him down at a day room table. The box is the intercom system in every cell.

They wanted everyone to see who might be ratting them out.

After an hour, they took him to the outside yard and left him there for another hour until he cracked.

He ended up snitching on three Mexicans, who the deputies came to collect later from the cell block. It was 4:00 a.m., but the whole cell block was wide awake, watching.

Nobody wants to be asleep and wake up to find their friends missing. Meanwhile, the Mexicans, drunk off pruno, were having a field day beating up the whites just for kicks.

Keep in mind, when the Mexicans are drunk, it's time to be on high alert for the inevitable riots that follow.

Sure enough, the next morning, there was one in cell block 6C, right next to ours. It involved the Bloods and the Crips.

I heard what sounded like a herd of buffalo thundering down the tier that's how bare feet sound in the cell block.

T-Rex and the other Crips who got rolled up from our cell block to cell block 6C Bear, Pookie, and Dookie

Stick—started it. When they got moved, they were sent to a Blood cell block, and the Bloods jumped T-Rex. But once he was back with his gang, T-Rex got his revenge. Remember, he's in for a murder on a Lincoln Park gangster, which is who they fought in the riot.

Lincoln Park gangsters fight well in here.

Lil Pookie, now known as Pretty Pookie because I said he looked like he was putting on deodorant after his scrap with Redrum, is also known to start riots. Word is Redrum likes to max out.

Maxing out means serving one's full sentence in jail or prison.

Pookie may be a pretty boy, but true gangsters can see that it's not a weakness; he'll do whatever it takes to prove he doesn't care.

That's how I became a real gangster forget being pretty; we can fight or shoot it out.

Today is just another day after yesterday. It began with a visit from

my daughter and grandson. I sat alone
in the visiting room for about ten
minutes, wondering who would be here
thinking about me so early in the
morning.

Then, around the corner of the
visiting room door, came my grandson.
He walked up to the visiting phone,
picked it up, and just stared at it.
I couldn't help but chuckle inwardly,
thinking, "Yeah, son, you don't want
to put that thing up to your face."

He smiled and flashed me a peace
sign. His grin was as wide as Ronald
McDonald's. Like all kids, he rushed
in to set the stage for his mother.
People often say we all look the same,
and in a way, we do we look good. They
came in from Texas.

"How are you doing, Dad?" she asked,
and the usual pleasantries followed.
Nevertheless, she also brought me bad
news, and for me, bad news always came
with a "Did you hear about..."

This time, it was about Reanna.
Whenever you hear that, it means the

person is dead. And, like always,
she was.

Reanna was my homegirl, like a
sister to me. But now, she was dead.
She was the sister of my homeboys
V-Dog and Mike B.

In the life of black people, some
individuals show you what it truly
means to be black, and she was one of
them.

I won't go into detail about how
she was killed, but it was the same
way her mother died in the late 80's.

I don't feel hurt because I've
been reading the Bible every day and
reflecting on death. The Bible teaches
that when you're dead, it's like the
light on a candle being extinguished—
it doesn't go anywhere; it's simply
put out.

Returning to the cell block after
my visit, I found three new gangsters
awaiting housing.

They sat at the blacks' table
looking visibly frightened.

One of them lacked shower shoes, and the atmosphere in the cell block felt peculiar, though oddities were nothing new to me.

They had no shower shoes because they had been involved in the riot next door, kicking them off in haste to either flee or engage in a fight.

Their reluctance to make eye contact marked them as Bloods to the inmates.

Most gang members from this cell block were relocated to the adjacent one, 6C, after the riot.

The Crips held some sway there.

Meanwhile, the Crips had devised plans to brutally assault a gang member involved in the riot, who now sat on the bench under the phones, barefoot and vulnerable.

Approaching me while I sat with Blood Killer, he asserted, "OG, I can scrap one-on-one, but I won't step into a cell."

I warned him sternly, "Don't think you'll walk out of here saying D-Man didn't say or do anything."

I emphasized, "Never come up to my table again." Blood Killer, visibly agitated, declared his intention to "stomp his brains out."

I cautioned him, "BK, don't get rolled up."

However, the gangster refused to retreat to his cell.

He opted to roam the cell block, a wise move until a Southsider recognized him as a riot instigator from Vista County jail.

The Mexicans issued a green light, a hit on him.

Realizing the danger, he voluntarily locked himself up, strategizing his next move.

Perhaps luck would have him reunited with his associates placed in a different cell block dominated by bloods.

Today marks the first of the year.

I received an outside visit from Mike, known as "nobody," one of the individuals from the outside who teaches me about the Bible.

I shared the news of Reanna's passing with him. He offered his condolences, saying, "Sorry to hear that, Derek."

I reassured him, "I'm okay. I find solace in what I read in the Bible you gave me last week. It compares the dead to a candle extinguished simply gone."

We delved into discussions about the Bible, and he guided me in understanding its teachings.

Learning comes naturally to me because I already believe I was sent here by God, which I confided in him.

After his visit, he offered a heartfelt prayer for me, to which I expressed it was the most meaningful prayer I've heard.

Back in the cell block, violence continued with more altercations. Box Head and his cellmate were rolled up for fighting. His cellmate, an East Coast Crip from L.A., was someone I had given a bag of Gold Pretzels to recently.

I punctured a hole in the bag to release the air and slid it under his cell door. I chuckled, "Nah, man, you're not hungry, you're thirsty. Three pretzels to one cup of water."

Later that day, he approached me, saying, "I got you for the pretzels, D-Man." I waved him off, replying, "Nah, pass it on to the next guy. I'm good."

Chapter 11

BLOOD KILLER PUTS ME UP

When the police took Box Head, Blood Killer tried to cover for them, claiming they were just play fighting. But the reality was Box Head was battling with the African inmate, who now sits in his cell with a target on his back.

He won't see the dawn. With two crip cellmates, Box Head, a West Coast crip, walks through the cell block flaunting his gang affiliation daily. This loss won't be brushed aside by anyone; Blood Killer ensures I stay in the loop.

Despite facing a murder beef, he keeps it close to the chest. He once told me, "If I can handle it in my sleep, I can handle anything." Now, he's the new shot caller for the crip car in Cell Block 6B. At this point, there's no black car only the bloods and the crips.

He warned me, "D-Man, if you refuse a fade in this block, I'll take you on myself."

I replied, "Alright, just make sure you don't get rolled up, I need you.

If you do, it'll set off a chain reaction." He assured me, "I won't, D-Man, I just won't." Now, he joins me at my table every day, silently observing the other inmates with his fist pressed against his face.

Later, during lockdown, piercing screams erupted from a Mexican inmate on the first tier, prompting deputies to rush to cell 133 in numbers. The inmate's cries echoed through the cell block, leading me to speculate on the cause—perhaps a broken limb from a brawl. However, the reality was grim; he had attempted suicide, and his desperate act had failed.

Three nurses swiftly entered the cell block, met with a chorus of jeers from the inmates. Upon surveying the scene, they hurriedly fetched a stretcher.

Amidst the continued wails of pain, they carefully lifted the naked inmate onto it and wheeled him out of the cell block.

The inmate lay hog-tied, his toes twitching as he lay on his stomach. Deputies forcibly grabbed his legs, slamming them against his back, yet he continued to scream and moan.

His attempted suicide stemmed from his desperate desire to move out of his solitary cell and into one with a cellmate.

The loneliness weighed heavily on him.

However, remaining in solitary confinement was crucial for asserting power and gaining more cells for one's own race.

These cells, equipped with two or three bunks, were highly coveted commodities.

Surrendering a cell meant conceding defeat, a game played not only by Mexicans but also by blacks and whites.

In the midst of this grim reality, Blood Killer orchestrated retaliation against the African inmate who had caused Box Head's punishment.

He dispatched a crip to confront the African, resulting in a lengthy brawl that left Blood Killer satisfied. Lil Nick was then tasked with retrieving the crip from the fray.

Lil Nick Dog remained unaware that his actions marked the initial stage of retaliation against him.

Each day would now become a battle until he inevitably landed in solitary confinement himself.

Yet, no one dared to provoke me. I've earned my stripes both in prison and on the streets, proving my loyalty to the gang.

When I ordered Lil Nick out of the cell block, he timidly inquired if he could relocate to cell 128.

The officers, sensing my authority, intervened, questioning if I had prior prison experience.

Acknowledging my history at San Quentin in the '80s, they promptly denied him permission to stay, citing my uncompromising nature.

As Lil Nick gathered his belongings to leave, I seized the opportunity to assert my dominance. With a warning scrawled on my new T-shirt, I made it clear that crossing me was not an option.

I harbor both a good and a bad side, the former enduring bullets for others while the latter vows to protect fiercely against any threat.

I had a clash with The Trolley Cop Killer, whose childish antics landed him in a new cell block.

He'd incessantly bang on our cell desk and door, particularly when I was trying to rest.

Under my blanket, I pondered the profound disrespect of his actions.

When I finally addressed him, warning him to cease, he remained silent a silent affirmation of his intent to defy. It's what you say to your crew later, after contemplating your defiance.

To make my stance crystal clear, I emerged from beneath my blanket and confronted him.

His retort echoed with defiance, but it was too late. I demanded he pack his belongings and summoned the deputies to remove him from my cell.

Two deputies quickly intervened and escorted him out.

He pleaded, "Can I please stay in the cell block?"

After dealing with the Trolley Cop Killer, I headed to the medical center for a TB shot.

Interestingly, the deputy who accompanied me was the same one who had removed the troublemaker from the cell block. He expressed gratitude, saying, "Thank you, D-Man, for not resorting to violence. That would have meant a lot of paperwork."

I replied, confessing that I had entertained thoughts of dragging him from the top bunk while he slept and ensuring he hit his head on the desk below.

I admitted that when such ideas crossed my mind, it was a sign that it was time for him to leave.

No paperwork necessary; I didn't harbor any hatred towards him. He was just a young man seeking attention in the wrong way. Leaving the medical center, I realized I had missed my chance to visit the chapel. However, it seemed that divine intervention was still on my side, offering me another opportunity to worship and seek forgiveness for my sins.

In the chapel, all the inmates approached me, expressing their gratitude for filing the grievance last week regarding our inability to leave the cell block for chapel services.

They said, "D-Man, thank you for advocating for us."

I acknowledged their appreciation, thanking them for trusting in my ability to address the issue.

Meanwhile, I found myself with a new cellmate, B-Nutty from Lincoln, who's an OG in his own right.

Ruben, also known as Drifter from El Cajon City, had a court appearance today to overturn the nine-year deal he had agreed to last month. He believed that because the deal seemed too good at nine years, the prosecution lacked sufficient evidence against him.

He felt confident in opting for a trial by jury, despite my advice that pleading guilty once would likely lead to a guilty verdict the second time around.

The Mexican shot callers assured him that he could beat his case if he chose to go to trial.

He recounted an incident at a party where a rival gang member confronted him, triggering his instinct to react by punching the individual in the eye, resulting in a broken eye socket.

He explained how the confrontation unfolded, saying, "He came into my space, D-Man." Understanding his perspective, I acknowledged, "I know.

I've been there too, and that's what we call great bodily injury."

His weary appearance didn't go unnoticed, his bloodshot eyes revealing his fatigue.

He mentioned, "Yeah, tomorrow I'll be going on a dry run." I cautioned him, "That's a tactic used by the DA to break down your perception of the truth.

Avoid eating the food in the court tank; it can soften your resolve and make you susceptible to taking any plea deal. Stay sharp." Grateful for the advice, he thanked me and went off to confer with some of his fellow gangsters.

I decided not to dwell on fighting today, as there were already too many instances to recount.

Meanwhile, back at court, the Southsiders' shot caller's cell became an impromptu MMA fighting ring.

Throughout the day, Mexican inmates were constantly streaming in and out of the cell, treating it like a cannabis store. During court runs, cell doors remained open, allowing for such chaos to ensue.

Chapter 12

FAMILIAR CONFINES OF JAIL

The following day unfolded peacefully, devoid of fights, arguments, or cell block disruptions. As for myself, my mind was occupied with thoughts about my case and how best to present it to my lawyer.

It had been 82 days since he last visited, and I eagerly anticipated our meeting. He had advised me not to discuss the details of my case, and I had adhered to his counsel thus far.

Reflecting on my circumstances, I couldn't help but ponder my past prayers for guidance in the streets. Ironically, within a matter of days,

I found myself back in the familiar confines of a jail cell.

It made me reconsider the efficacy of praying in the streets; sometimes, you might just get what you wish for. Perhaps, in sending me back to jail, God was guiding me home, redirecting my search for answers from the streets to within myself.

In essence, I realized that I had been searching for something in the streets that I could not find there. Turning to spiritual literature like Our Daily Bread provided solace and perspective during these uncertain times.

Every day, I find solace and guidance in the words of Our Daily Bread. Today's message struck an accord with me: "If you're in a locked-in syndrome, why not prayerfully reflect on some ways you can still reach out to others?"

It served as a reminder of the power of connection and outreach, even in challenging circumstances.

My time here has given me a newfound appreciation for the freedoms and privileges I once took for granted.

One such privilege was having my girl by my side during visits. However, today's visit took an unexpected turn from the start.

I innocently inquired about my son, hoping for any news she might have.

Yet, her response carried an undertone of indifference, leaving me feeling dismissed and insignificant. It seemed as though my concerns were trivial compared to her own. Attempting to glean information about my legal proceedings only elicited further disregard.

She visibly shut down any conversation that didn't revolve around her, leaving me feeling isolated and invalidated.

Seeing her alone for the visit, I couldn't help but feel a pang of disappointment. It was as if her presence, once a source of comfort, now felt underwhelming and inadequate.

When she expressed her eagerness to leave, citing her own problems, I couldn't help but feel a sense of abandonment.

I tried to catch her gaze, but she avoided eye contact, claiming she needed to take her daughter to the bus stop.

With a heavy heart, I shared the news of my homegirl's passing, hoping for some solace or acknowledgment.

Instead, she offered to chant, a response that left me feeling hollow and unheard.

Back in the cell block, the weight of my reality crashed down on me once again.

Exhausted, I retreated to my cell, seeking refuge in solitude as I contemplated my circumstances.

It struck me how my girl resented any connection I had with others outside of her realm. She discouraged expressions of love for my family and criticized my attempts to reach out to them.

As I woke from my nap, these thoughts weighed heavily on my mind. Despite my efforts to support fellow inmates, I couldn't shake the absence of love in my heart. I questioned whether their faith in me was genuine or merely borne out of fear.

But upon reflection, I realized the true source of discord lay with my girl, whose lack of faith and self-centeredness cast a shadow over our relationship.

I felt a surge of anger when she offered to chant for my deceased friend.

Reflecting on it now, writing this story has allowed me to confront my emotions and speak my truth, bringing me a sense of relief. Later in the day, as I carried out my duties as a worker, I found solace in conversing with other inmates in the cell block about my experiences.

Sharing my story brought me a sense of catharsis. I attribute my newfound peace to the trials I've faced and the lessons I've learned during my time in lockdown. Visiting the jail chapel regularly has been a source of comfort and enlightenment for me.

During one of these discussions, Blue Light asked me about writing a book. I explained that for me, writing was a way to tell my own story, almost like composing my own obituary.

When the police threatened my life, I felt compelled to share my truth with the world, to ensure that my story was known.

"They wouldn't kill me for nothing," I assured him. "It's doing well. Have you read my latest news and literature clips?" "No, actually, I haven't even read the old ones," he admitted.

I fetched the entire pack from my cell, assuring him he could return it later.

Later arrived, and after he perused the 20 or 30 news articles on ONEIGHTYSEVEN, he seemed impressed.

He marveled at the idea of a gangster achieving something like a published book.

"He thought I was shooting for the stars and hit," I chuckled.

"My publisher's already waiting for the next one."

When I went to retrieve my news clips from his cell, his cellmate, who had been sitting on his bunk, spoke up.

"D-Man, I read your book at school," he said.

"Yeah?" I replied.

"Hell yeah," he exclaimed. "I read about you and your homeboy V-Dog when you ran with the west coast."

He mentioned he had read it at San Diego High School in the library. Interestingly, his cellmate was the same gangster who had clashed with The Trolley Cop Killer.

The day after his altercation with the Trolley Cop Killer, I decided to extend an olive branch by sliding a pack of Oreo cookies under his cell door.

Catching him in the midst of a set of pushups, I figured a snack would be appreciated after a workout.

The following morning, we were served eggs and hash browns for breakfast, a hearty meal to kickstart the day and pack on some weight.

As the day progressed, we remained on edge due to the looming threat of a week-long lockdown for a visit from high-ranking officials.

Throughout the day, the deputies kept me busy cleaning the cell block longside two other inmates. While everyone else was locked down by 10:30 PM, I didn't finish until 1:00 AM.

Despite the late hour, I welcomed the chance for a shower to help me unwind and sleep.

Despite our efforts, we failed the cell inspection, resulting in the loss of our TV privileges.

However, we managed to get through the visit, albeit with some setbacks. The morning announcement blared over the loudspeaker, delivering the news of our failed inspection and the consequent 24-hour loss of TV privileges. It was a disappointing start to the day for all of us.

Venturing outside for the first time in what felt like ages, I soaked up the warmth of the sunlight on my skin, which had paled from being cooped up in the cell block 24/7.

As I removed my shirt, curious eyes turned to me, with the Mexicans marveling at my physique and asking how I got so big. I shrugged modestly, attributing it to regular push-ups and expressing a desire to bulk up even more if I had the opportunity.

Peering between the razor wire fences separating cell block 5 and 6, I caught a glimpse of Donovan State Prison in the distance. Despite my vision impairment from a past gunshot wound to the head, I could still discern the sharp points of the razor wire at the fence's summit.

Though I had left my glasses behind in the cell block, the scene before me was clear enough to remind me of the barriers and boundaries that defined our confinement.

Chapter 13

O'FARRELL PARK BLOOD GANG

It was a routine occurrence. Later that evening, I joined Fruit Town, his cellmate Baby Sleep, along with two white inmates, Jay from the Lakeside gangsters, and Remmer, for bible study.

Baby Sleep, hailing from the O'Farrell Park blood gang, recounted his brush with death after being shot by the police, expressing gratitude for his survival.

Standing in a circle, we clasped hands and offered our prayers.

Then, we delved into the sermon delivered by Jay, who read from Samuel 11 Chapter 1.

The story he recounted was so compelling that it left me transfixed, with my bible in one hand and the other resting by my side, as if I were standing at attention.

I locked eyes with Jay as he recounted the powerful tale.

After the sermon, Baby Sleep exclaimed, recognizing me as Derek Grover from Bloccide, the author of ONEIGHTYSEVEN.

Silence fell over the cell block as all eyes turned to me.

I acknowledged the recognition with gratitude, feeling affirmed for the work I do.

Baby Sleep gripped my hand firmly, refusing to let go, as others in the circle attributed the encounter to the power of God.

Reflecting on the story Jay had shared from the Bible, about King David going to battle in the spring, resonated deeply with me.

As a former gang leader accustomed to the rigors of conflict, the parallels were striking.

Later that night, Baby Sleep visited my cell, and we delved into discussions about our past lives on the streets.

He confided in me, expressing regrets about not staying home with his pregnant wife.

His words, written on my legal pad, served as a stark reminder of the realities of street life, resonating far beyond our conversation.

I'm Baby Sleep form O'Farrell Park, what made me educate myself was my brother, Lil Sleepy Bo passing away. I realized I had to educate myself in order to succeed. The average black youth fail to realize education is everything and knowledge is the true power that you need to accomplish positive goals in life. I want others young black males to realize in order to be successful in this world we need to seek self, improvement and education and guidance from Jesus

Christ. I thank the Lord for giving me the opportunity to enlighten you and giving me the opportunity to still wake up and breath because I should have been dead numerous times. Life is a struggle but there is hope through God. Thanks to the G homie Derek Grover for this opportunity.

Baby Sleep from O'Farrell Park.

Later that night took a turn for the worse. It all began after the night count when a new inmate entered the cell block.

He was as black as tar, towering at 6'8" and look like 380 pounds, with a rugged beard resembling a grizzly bear.

I peered out of my cell door, adamant that this behemoth wouldn't be placed in my cell.

He sat at one of the blacks' table, awaiting assignment.

I remained vigilant throughout the night, refusing to rest.

If he dared to approach my cell, I was ready to unleash fury.

However, during count, Deputy Wilson, a black officer, entered for the count. When he reached my cell, I voiced my concern, bluntly stating that I didn't want the new inmate in my cell.

My words were sharp, laced with frustration and defiance.

He exclaimed, "What the fuck is wrong with you? Goddamn!"

I stood my ground, emphasizing that I wasn't joking and gestured as if I had a gun to his head.

"You better radio the control booth and tell them my shit is rolled up," I insisted, clearing the path for him to see my belongings packed in brown paper bags.

Deputy Wilson questioned if I knew the new inmate. "No, but he won't be shitting, snoring, and farting in my cell like he's in the woods," I retorted, maintaining my stance.

As he walked away, he advised me to chill the fuck out, noting my excessive energy.

I thanked him and reclined on my bunk. An hour later, I awoke and sought forgiveness from God through prayer, acknowledging my lapse in judgment.

Reflecting on the incident, I considered it a test from God, one that I had failed. I resolved to seek further guidance from the Word of God, believing that I could fare better on the streets with the right mindset.

But what I seek is within these walls. The following morning greeted us with French toast for breakfast, a sweet beginning to the day.

Sunday, chapel day, holds a special significance here.

It's a beacon of hope amidst the routine. Today, we were graced by three chaplains, each delivering messages that resonated deeply.

The chapel was packed, a rare sight, with seemingly every San Diego

killer in attendance, especially those
who've been apprehended.

   As I stirred from my evening nap,
the guard's voice pierced through,
signaling the final call for church. I
sprang off my bunk and hit the button
on my call box.

   "What?" the guard's voice crackled.
"Open my cell door for church," I
replied, hearing the electric lock
disengage in response.

   Still half-asleep, I slipped into my
shower shoes.

   Here, like in any jail, shoes
or tennis shoes are prohibited,
during fights they provide an unfair
advantage.

   Barefooted, you stand and fight. All
you hear are the sounds of feet and
fists meeting flesh. After rubbing the
sleep from my eyes, I stepped onto the
tier with the Bible in hand.

Chapter 14

SHOT 20 TIMES WITH AN AK-47

I left my glasses behind, rendering
the text of the Bible unreadable.
So, I simply held it in my hand and
absorbed the message of the day.

The feeling of anticipation that
fills me is one I don't want to fade.
Each day, I see signs of God's work
within me, and I believe my fellow
inmates can see it too.

God has equipped me with everything
necessary to face my case head-on.
Come Thursday, I'll attend my
Readiness Conference to prepare for
next week's Preliminary Hearing.

Yesterday, as I glanced through my
cell door, I spotted a Filipino inmate

dressed in all greens, the attire reserved for lifers. He had his bed roll under his arm.

He was just pacing the cell block floor. He kept at it for about an hour and a half, until they finally popped my cell door.

Once it was open, I made my way downstairs and settled onto the bench by the phone for a moment, and he approached close enough for us to have a conversation.

I gestured for him to come closer, and he obliged.

"What race are you?" I inquired. He replied, "Filipino." I asked because he could have passed for Mexican.

"Are you waiting to be housed?" I questioned further. He confirmed, adding, "Yes, but I can't be housed with any other race than Filipino."

"Is that right?" I mused. "Yeah," he affirmed.

I clarified, "If you're Filipino, you can be housed with a black."

He nodded, acknowledging the rule.

"What's your name?" I queried. "Smiley," he responded.

"Smiley, are you the gangster who shot me 20 times with an AK-47 in my dream last week?" I jested.

He chuckled, "No, but I got an attempted murder, that's why I'm wearing the greens."

Surprised, I remarked, "I've never heard of that, wearing greens with no conviction."

He agreed, stating he felt the same way. Just then, the deputy called his name and escorted him out of the cell block. We shook hands before he returned to his gangster homies.

Later, a Lakeside gangster approached me, expressing his admiration for the way blacks handle fights one on one, no rat packs involved.

"But the Mexicans and the whites," he continued, "they do it differently, rat pack style." Pointing at Jeff, he illustrated his point.

Jeff, battered and bruised, was limping had two black eyes, broke fingers, exercising doing pushups despite his injuries, a testament to the brutal nature of prison fights.

Later that day, I got a new cellmate.

Having been alone for six days, I was expecting the change, but not just anyone could move in.

"What's up, homie? I'm D-Man from Bloccide crips," I introduced myself.

"Where you from?" "I'm Turtle, from the Brims," he replied.

"It's cool," I said, removing my glasses. "But if you're bringing that blood stuff into my cell, you need to leave now."

"Wait a minute, OG," he responded quickly. "I don't bang." "Neither do I," I assured him.

But these niggas in here do, and I can't prevent them from bringing it to my cell. However, I can make sure it doesn't leave.

You don't have to worry about that with me. I'm 31 years old and know how to respect others. He mentioned he was informed on the first tier that all the Bloods were upstairs.

I confirmed, saying, "That's right, all but me.

So, if you think they can't touch you, think again because I'm here." I emphasized that as long as we understood each other, we'd be fine.

He remarked, "Damn, I was thinking it's on like that," implying that situations escalate quickly in here.

Nonetheless, we were cool.

As a gesture of peace, I gave him a 30.9 power-up anti-perspirant deodorant stick. Later in the day, I attended the Catholic Church service and approached Chaplain Joe, seeking guidance on how to stop this conflict.

He reassured me, saying, "God will forgive you 70 x 7 and forever for your sins."

He also mentioned, "But that is bad, Grover. You need to stop and think about what you are doing."

I assured him, "I will stop, and I will tell them Chaplain Joe told me to stop."

Last night, I couldn't sleep because I was contemplating my case. I thought of several good points to bring up at my court hearing on Thursday.

It will be my Readiness Conference, where my attorney, the D.A., and the judge will engage in open bargaining.

I won't be accepting any deals on my case because whenever I end up in jail, it's always because the police want me in prison, whether I'm guilty or not.

Last week, I received a police report.

The USB stick provided by the D.A. to my attorney was corrupt. Anyway, the Mexicans are at it again with the alcohol, completely wasted.

The cell block feels more like a Mexican gangster bar these days.

The police keep warning everyone to stay in their cells because of the alcohol. It feels like a Monday night Chargers game with the Raiders, and the inmates are cheering like fans, holding Charger mugs filled with beer.

The guards are patrolling with their 12-inch flashlights tucked into their pants leg pockets.

Turtle left today, but before he did, he mentioned how many inmates' mothers are driving them downtown to the police department to snitch on their homies.

It wasn't news to me, but it was good to see him go. That's two guys out in one week from this cell.

My cell now resembles an office, with all my case papers spread across the two empty bunks.

Derek Grover

Late last night, I started feeling flu-like symptoms and went to the MTA for medical attention.

I returned to the cell block at 1:00 am, with only three hours of sleep before my court appearance at 8:30 am.

It all began with the lengthy wait in the court tank, where every inmate in the jail was gathered for the bus ride into downtown San Diego.

This process alone takes four hours and can really wear you down.

Once downtown, we're placed into another set of tanks to wait until every inmate from all the other jails are grouped with us, which takes an additional three hours.

Chapter 15

SOME REAL G-SHIT

At that moment, I knew I would see my crime partner Al-Dog, and sure enough, he was placed into the court tank next to mine.

I called out to him, hoping he could be placed in my tank, but before I knew it, the first freed-up deputy had us cuffed together and placed in the same tank.

Once in court, I shared my paperwork with him since his lawyer hadn't provided him with any.

My attorney brought good news for me, but unfortunately, Al-Dog's attorney only brought bad news for him. Despite our differences in legal

representation, we were both put off
for two weeks when we spoke to the
judge.

Nevertheless, it was reassuring
to have our people in court showing
support for us. At that moment, Al-Dog
seemed downcast and confused about
the situation.

While he grappled with his
emotions, I couldn't help but feel
optimistic that my time to go home for
good, without bail, was approaching.

Later that day, Al-Dog was released
he bailed out.

During the bus ride home, the
inmates filled the air with the lyrics
of "Ain't No Sunshine when you go
home" playing on the radio. Upon our
return to the cell block, tension hung
heavy in the air once again.

My neighbor in the cell next to
mine is from Lincoln, but I won't
dignify him by mentioning his name in
my writings.

This guy holds a 15-year ticket but
hardly ever steps out of his cell.

When the guards initially attempted
to house him with the crips, he was
met with a stern warning that entering
our cell would make him fair game.

Faced with this threat, he opted
to perch himself on the phone bench
draped in a white jailhouse blanket,
pounding away on the bench till the
early hours of the morning.

Ultimately, he ended up being
housed with a younger inmate.

During breakfast this morning, his
cellmate began banging on the chow
hall table at 4:20 am.

I glanced up and firmly told him to
cut it out. All eyes in the cell block
turned towards me.

Sensing the need for a
conversation, I called the youngster
over. He's a blood, but none of the
bloods were willing to mentor him.

They deferred to me, saying, "You do
it, D-Man."

So, I took on the responsibility.
As a fellow black inmate, I felt

I could connect with him in a way others couldn't. I imparted some wisdom about navigating life in jail, and he listened attentively, showing great respect. From that moment on, I instructed him to sit beside me during all three meals. And during dinner, as he returned from court, he took his place at my table.

However, Blood Killer, claiming ownership of the seat as a "general," confronted the young gangster.

The youngster, respecting his authority, began to gather his food to move.

Blood Killer's response was, "That's okay for now," as he walked away, then turned back to the youngster and cautioned, "I told you, it's no joke in here.

You need to be put up on the truth. Your homeboys are not telling you." Later in the day, Redrum approached me and commented, "D-Man, you act like you're the youngsters' daddy."

Meeting his gaze squarely, I replied, "I am the niggas' daddy."

The youngster was from the Brims. Redrum acknowledged, "That's some real G-shit, D-Man."

I noted that although he was affiliated with the blood car, I ensured he and his cellmate received their food trays and escorted them to their cell, leaving the youngster to fend for himself.

Hence, the table banging after every meal. Redrum seemed displeased by this truth, but as they say, the truth hurts.

He also suggested, "D-Man, you could have pulled the young homie to the side and told him."

I explained, "I told him in front of the cell block so everyone would know."

"I'm going to address the bad habits he's picking up," I declared.

He seemed hesitant, so I asked, "Would you like me to water it down?"

He stammered, but I pressed on, asking, "Who is the leader of the blood car?

Business will be going home on the 25th; it's going to be a loss for your car." Fruit Towns from Los Angeles; the crips don't concern him, this is San Diego," I emphasized.

He continued, "The crips came to me and asked, 'Are you going to let the O.G. homie check your homeboy?'"

I interpreted it as a warning that they're coming for him sooner rather than later.

"It's a test of the blood car's power," I explained. Blood Killer shared that he had sent someone to test them, and they had failed.

He's determined to live up to his name, wanting to dismantle the blood car during his tenure.

The next day, four gangsters were placed in our cell block, two bloods and two non-affiliated. One of them came to my cell.

Derek Grover

I heard the announcement over the loudspeaker: "Go to cell 228." Without hesitation, I moved to stand by my cell door slot, where I had placed my dead homegirl's obituary.

It was my way of signaling that I was in mourning and not to be messed with.

The obituary faced outward on my cell's glass window, ensuring everyone knew my state of mind.

I made it clear to everyone that we were all in mourning together.

The new inmate approached my cell door, pausing to peer inside.

Although the second tier was designated for the bloods, I, as a non-affiliated member, had the freedom to choose my cellmate.

When the guard opened my cell door, the new inmate entered and shut it behind him. Stepping forward, I greeted him, "What's up, homie? I'm D-Man.

What's your name?"

His response didn't register with me; his name wasn't important.

Instead, I asked, "Where are you from?" He replied, "Skyline." I told him straight up, "It's cool, but if you bring any drama in here, I'll toss you over the tier."

He assured me he wasn't about to start any trouble.

Within ten minutes, another inmate, sent by the deputy, joined us, making it three in the cell. I began to contemplate whether it was time for me to move down to the first tier with the crips. And that's exactly what I did.

As I entered the first tier, I was greeted with welcoming words: "Welcome back, general."

They assigned me to cell 128, Bear's old cell and a Mexican gangster from Sherman Heights explained to me that "128" is for making prison complaints.

Later that day, I returned to the second tier to inform everyone about my move downstairs.

I stopped by Mark's cell, my white homeboy from Lakeside gangsters, who was facing a murder charge. He had killed his girlfriend in a downtown hotel, stuffed her body in a suitcase, and dumped her in the trash bin.

Mark showed me his cellmate's imitation of me, and we shared a moment of laughter amidst the chaos of prison life.

Chapter 16

BECAUSE YOU LIKE KILLING

I nodded, signaling approval. His cellmate mimicked me, gesturing as if he were putting others in check, using his index and middle finger like a gun, in Marks face.

On the first night in my new cell, I woke up feeling irritable. During breakfast, Bam from the East Coast Crips in Los Angeles asked if our cellmate was going to eat. I responded sharply, expressing my indifference with a fuck that nigga.

Bam turned to our other cellmate, Nick Dog from the Coast, and asked the same question. Despite my dismissive attitude, Nick Dog went to wake up our cellmate so he could eat.

Eventually, our cellmate emerged and hurried to the food cart to collect his tray. Later, I noticed all the crips standing outside their cells, dozens deep and standing at attention.

Baby Durk inquired about the newspaper, and when told it was upstairs in my old cell, 228, he volunteered to retrieve it.

I asked if anyone wanted me to go. Despite not fully hearing the response, I proceeded anyway. Baby Durk approached cell 127 and inquired about the newspaper.

As I stood over him, I observed a gangster reading it inside the cell. However, from my bunk downstairs, I saw a Brim take a paper to his cell.

Realizing the paper was likely in my old cell, 228, I headed there and found everyone reading it.

Knocking on the door, I demanded the paper. Despite their claims that

it had been sent downstairs to Blood
Killer, I insisted, raising my voice.

When they hesitated, I intensified
my demand, implying consequences
if they didn't comply. Blood Killer
eventually intervened, confirming that
the paper was indeed downstairs.
Feeling frustrated, I walked away,
expressing my displeasure.

Shortly after, the deputy called
Blood Killer to the gate. Blood Killer
was directed to attend the PHC, but he
couldn't understand why.

"Why do I need to see the doctor?"
he questioned, baffled by the order. The
deputy's response was curt: "Because
you like killing people."

Blood Killer, along with Lil
Durk, was escorted away. Meanwhile,
when asked about his well-being, I
admitted, "I need help too."

Surprised, they probed further, and
I found himself in a razor wire cage
in the yard outside the cell block at
night, pouring out my concerns. "I'm
too strong," I confessed. "I think
people are scared of me. I have a

short fuse and feel I can fuck up everyone in the cell block."

The crips are calling me "the General," a departure from the previous moniker, G-block.

"I need help," I concluded. The next morning loomed with apprehension as court day approached.

I wasn't keen on attending, anticipating a grim outcome.

Court days always commenced early, with wake-up calls as early as 4:00 am, signaling the start of an arduous day ahead.

You'll be rushed through breakfast and then sent to the court tanks for several hours, where all the prisoners going to court across the jail convene.

It's here that you will encounter your enemies. In my case, I spotted a gangster I'd had issues with before. Despite the tension, I wasted no time. "Get ready for the scrap," I warned him, sensing his readiness despite his silence. But my attitude didn't go unnoticed by the guard, who asked for my inmate ID number.

In my agitated state, I fumbled, blurting out some random digits, 000187. Sensing trouble, the guard swiftly removed me from the tank and transferred me to a different one in the medical ward.

"You'll be going to court in the van, by yourself," he informed me.

I shrugged it off, attributing my terse response to not being a morning person.

Upon arriving at court, my attorney delivered unexpected news: the presence of a news crew, possibly recording my case for the next day's paper.

He remarked, "Wouldn't that be nice."

My case had already made headlines, so another news feature wasn't a big deal. Court proceedings went smoothly, but the outcome wouldn't be revealed until my next appearance in ten days.

Returning to the court tanks meant navigating through the stairwell in the old county jail, still rife with tension between the Bloods and Crips from the 80's.

Coincidentally, I encountered the gangster I'd previously clashed with. As we found ourselves placed together in a holding tank by the deputy, tensions flared.

The gangster entered the cell first, shedding his shower shoes, followed by me. Wordlessly, he attempted to sucker punch me, but his aim was off.

It was clear he wasn't itching for a fight. Nonetheless, I remained composed, knowing I could both take and deliver a hit if necessary.

After his initial punch, he seemed paralyzed with shock. Seizing the moment, I swiftly lifted him and slammed him into the corner of the holding cell before he could comprehend my next move. He stumbled around, unable to formulate a defense.

Once more, I hoisted him off the ground and carried him towards the toilet, intending to slam him into it.

But before I could, the deputy intervened, wrapping me up. Despite this, I managed to slam him onto the ground, asserting dominance.

He undoubtedly felt the force of my power.

However, the situation escalated rapidly as around 20 deputies flooded into the holding cell, overwhelmingly outnumbering me. They forcibly separated us, subjecting me to a barrage of blows from all angles.

As I lay on the ground, struggling to remain conscious, a deputy relentlessly kicked me, inflicting further pain.

It felt surreal, like I was trapped in a dream. The chokehold, wielded like a powerful pry bar, had forcefully intervened to quell the fight. Afterward, they segregated us, placing us in cells opposite each other.

It was a strange feeling, but somehow satisfying.

Later that night, I was roused from sleep by the sergeant's voice crackling over the intercom.

He queried whether I had lost consciousness during the deputy's chokehold. Uncertain, I replied that I believed I had, but it felt like I was caught in a dream, grappling with fragmented memories of being slammed against the wall.

Attempting to shake off the haze of sleep, I explained that I thought I had merely been dreaming about the incident.

The sergeant seemed to accept my response and fell silent.

It was a reminder of the constant surveillance within the confines of the cell block, where every moment seemed to be under scrutiny.

Chapter 17

BRUISED AND SWOLLEN

Once news spread about the altercation and my subsequent takedown by the deputies, I became somewhat of a legend among the inmates. They looked at me as if I were some kind of superhero and were eager to hear every detail of the encounter.

"Damn, OG, you act like that shit didn't even faze you?" they exclaimed, their curiosity piqued.

They clamored to inspect any visible bruises or marks, eager for evidence of the skirmish.

I obliged, opening my mouth to reveal my bruised and swollen tongue, marked with the distinct imprint of

my teeth. It resembled a horseshoe,
a testament to the forceful pressure
exerted during the struggle.

Then, I gestured towards my back,
pointing out the darkened patches
where I had been pummeled and kicked
while restrained on the ground.

I described the relentless assault,
the handcuffs and leg chains offering
no protection from the blows.

As I recounted the chaos, I
admitted that in the heat of the
moment, it felt like I was amidst a
riot, with the Mexicans, imagining
each strike as the thrust of a blade.

With my face pressed against the
ground, I was blind to the onslaught
behind me. Reflecting on the aftermath,
I remarked humorously that my back
resembled that of a runaway slave
who had stumbled upon the master's
house with stolen pigs in each arm a
vivid metaphor for the severity of the
beating I endured.

I shared with them that I don't
engage in masturbation and that
my testosterone levels were high,

contributing to my sense of strength. Despite the ordeal, I expressed relief at being returned to my original cell block and my willingness to move past the incident.

The other inmates were eager to assist me in any way they could, asking what they could do for me.

I simply requested some Ibuprofen, which they promptly provided, with each racial group contributing to help me feel better.

Throughout the day, they sought my guidance on how to toughen up and emulate my resilience.

I began training them, imparting lessons on resilience and mental toughness.

I reminded them of the childhood adage: if you cried when you fell off your bike, you couldn't take a punch, but if you didn't, you could.

Despite waking up stiff and sore the next day, I found solace in the camaraderie and support of my fellow inmates.

Things seemed to be aligning positively once more.

Furthermore, my cellmate Nick Dogg was released that morning, a welcomed development.

In his place, I gained a new cellmate, HC, a gangster from Westside Oceanside, who proved to be a pleasant addition to our cell.

I had a visit last night from Mike, also known as Nobody, my Jehovah's Witness Bible study teacher from the streets.

I confided in him about the altercation with the deputies and how the crips were attempting to recruit me as their leader.

Mike offered a perspective that resonated deeply with me.

He likened the challenges I faced to a scenario where the devil was relentlessly targeting me, akin to someone using a magnifying glass to burn an ant.

In this analogy, I was the ant, and the devil's focus was aimed at keeping me ensnared in his grasp.

He emphasized how the devil's actions were a mockery of God, which left me feeling disheartened at my perceived failure in the eyes of my faith.

I found solace in Mike's words as they echoed the inner turmoil I had been experiencing.

He described my situation as being trapped in a smoke-filled room, where others remained oblivious to the danger while I fought desperately to break free.

This metaphor perfectly encapsulated the sense of isolation and struggle I felt in my current circumstances.

In my case, the room is filled with gangsters, and I'm fighting to break free.

It's as if they can't see that gangbanging is destroying us from within. I've kept this internal struggle bottled up, hesitant to put it into words. But in the next few days, I've made the decision to tell Blood Killer that I'm done. I want no part in criminal activity anymore.

The fact that I wasn't sent to solitary confinement is reassurance that I'm still viewed favorably in the eyes of God.

During the ordeal when I was hog-tied, all I prayed for was the opportunity to continue writing my story, hoping that it could serve as a lesson for the youth.

I'm grateful for the chance to pray more, to immerse myself in the Word of God, and to worry less. My new purpose is to guide others towards righteousness in the eyes of God.

I find solace in this newfound path where I treat everyone with respect, free from the looming threat of violence. A few days ago, I had a conversation with Baby Sleep about a dispute he had with Business over a card game.

According to Baby Sleep, Business approached him aggressively during the game. Feeling challenged, Baby Sleep, who prides himself as a true rider for the blood car, suggested taking the issue to their cell, and Business agreed.

But upon arriving at the cell, Business hesitated, leading Baby Sleep to criticize him and question his courage, labeling his crew as nothing but a group of smokers.

It takes a lot of bravery to speak so boldly.

Despite Baby Sleep's taunts, Business remained silent, only threatening to fight him. Unfazed, Baby Sleep brushed it off. Fruit Town is Baby Sleep cellmate, he said, "I'm going to fuck that nigga up D-Man."

The clash between Baby Sleep and Business, the original 300, ended on an anticlimactic note. I reminded Baby Sleep that such confrontations don't sit well with God, urging him to steer clear of any further conflicts.

He's already facing serious charges for attempted murder on the police, with allegations that he fired shots at them, resulting in a retaliation that nearly cost him his life.

I shared with him how God had prompted me to recount my experience in the court tanks. I emphasized that it was by God's grace that I hadn't been thrown into solitary confinement after the fight.

Reflecting on the incident, I realized that I wasn't ready for change, especially since I had been threatening others with violence.

However, I knew it wasn't too late to turn things around. I urged him to do the same if he ever hoped to improve his situation.

I conveyed to him that this message came directly from God, and he admitted feeling similarly inclined.

It became clear to me that it was my duty to convey these words in the name of God, just as I had written ONEIGHTSEVEN under His guidance.

I made sure he understood the gravity of the situation, and he expressed his gratitude, acknowledging my authenticity.

As the night drew to a close, I found myself gazing into the mirror, contemplating my journey.

Despite the challenges, I couldn't help but yearn for the familiarity of the second tier.

Every other day, inmates on the second tier convened for a Bible study session. We'd rotate reading verses and offer prayers together.

One day, glancing over to a corner of the cell block, I initially mistook a gathering of Southsiders for a typical spread—a small meal symbolizing gang solidarity.

Upon closer inspection, I realized they were engaged in their own Bible study session.

Chapter 18

PULLING THE TRIGGER

I retrieved my Bible from my cell and positioned myself about five yards away from the Southsiders. As I began to read, a fellow black inmate approached me, suggesting I join their study. This was the same person I had adamantly opposed sharing my cell with.

Glancing at the Southsiders, I asked if it would be alright for me to study with them, to which they warmly agreed.

Taking a seat on the ground, I became part of their group, which comprised seven Southsiders and two whites, who preferred to be called "woods."

The reading progressed in a clockwise fashion, with each member taking turns reading aloud. It was a harmonious circle, drawing curious glances from others in the cell block.

The focus of our study centered on the principles of loving all races equally and embracing forgiveness.

The Southsider leading the study did an admirable job, and when called upon to speak, I joined in without hesitation.

I expressed to him, "Homie, I've got a lot of heart, but one thing I don't enjoy is reading out loud."

He reassured me, "You're doing a good job. I understand everything you're saying."

Despite his heavy Mexican accent, his message was crystal clear to the last word. I felt grateful for this group of Mexicans.

Just a few days prior, I thought
I was caught up in a riot with the
Southsiders, only to realize it was
the deputies.

Now, I found myself in a Bible
study with Southsides. As the session
concluded, they invited anyone in need
of a special prayer.

Each one eagerly responded, and I
was honored when asked to lead the
group in prayer.

We formed a circle, holding hands,
as I offered a prayer, mentioning
everyone's specific needs.

Following this, Nick Dogg was
instructed to roll up as he was headed
home. In his place, my new cellmate
arrived from the hole at Vista County
Jail in Oceanside. Young Loc, a member
of the 47th Street gang, found himself
incarcerated for murder.

He was also involved in the Crips'
clash with the Lincoln Park Bloods in
cell block 6C.

The catalyst for the riot was Don
Deigo from Lincoln, who pilfered 30

single-edge razors from the trash
during pill line, akin to having 30
Glocks in jail.

He distributed these razors to
every Blood in the cell block.

Young Loc boasted about photos of
him murdering a Lincoln Park gang
member outside Dr. J's liquor store,
which led to his transfer to Vista.
However, he was eventually returned to
George Bailey after inciting another
riot in Vista over a cookie.

Upon entering my cell, he
introduced himself, saying, "What up
homie, I'm Young Loc, neighborhood
Crip."

I replied, "I'm D-Man from Bloccide
Crips 187. But I took a beatdown from
the police. I can't move."

I was still sore under my blanket.

He mentioned that the homie next
door, referring to Blood Killer, had
to fight. He paced back and forth in
the cell.

I pulled the cover from over my head and stared at him, wanting him to meet my gaze as he spoke. But all he kept saying was, "Yeah, yeah, yeah."

Five minutes later, our cell door popped open and he dashed into Blood Killer's cell. I took off my shirt and began doing pushups.

I heard Blood Killer's cell door banging back and forth.

As I stepped out of my cell, I saw 36 crips standing outside. I walked towards Blood Killer's cell, but Baby Durk stopped me, saying, "Stay back, D-Man. Just this once."

I returned to doing pushups in front of the 36 gang members of the Crip car, beaten up badly. The fight lasted a grueling 4 minutes, though time holds little significance in here, that's still a long time.

Young Loc emerged from the cell first, a few drops of blood staining his T-shirt as he tended to cuts around his eyes.

I assumed Blood Killer had gotten the better of him. Then, Blood Killer followed, looking no better. They appeared as if they'd been through a meat grinder.

Young Loc asked me if I had a fresh T-shirt. I didn't, but I offered him a fresh blue shirt. He put it on and returned to the cell block. Meanwhile, Blood Killer headed to the general's table to play cards. Later, I had another Bible study with the Southsiders.

It was a peaceful gathering, but for me, it was a test of my faith.

Being the only non-Southsider in the group, I felt the tension.

The Black inmates were giving me strange looks, but they know I have conviction and was simply following my beliefs in God.

I explained to the Southsiders that for me, it wasn't that simple.

Look at my people I might have to fight them tonight.

But the desire to study with others
is too strong.

Fortunately, nothing escalated,
and I'm relieved. No one said a word.
Perhaps I should consider starting a
Bible study for the Black inmates.

Young Loc shared a story from his
youth. He recounted how, at 13 years
old, he and his friends went to a
liquor store in El Cajon city.

Driven by a desire to prove his
loyalty to his gang, he noticed he
was being recorded on the store's
surveillance system while chatting
with other customers at the counter.

After buying some candy, he stepped
outside and spotted a Blood gangster
dressed in red. Despite his young age,
his older friends handed him a pistol.

He recounted how he boldly
approached the Blood gangsters,
greeting them with a casual "what's
up, blood" before brandishing the
pistol.

He described the Blood gangster's eyes widening in shock as he pointed the gun at them.

He admitted to pulling the trigger, expecting the loud bang of gunfire, but nothing happened.

Frustrated, he kept squeezing the trigger repeatedly, but still, there was no sound, and the Blood gangster fled in fear.

Young Loc then ran back to his friends, informing them of the malfunctioning gun.

He expressed his anger, describing the situation as if the gun was malfunctioning due to the rain or some other factor.

He handed the gun back to his friend, confirming that it was indeed jammed. He described a moment when a car turned the corner, and bullets whizzed through the air as the vehicle passed by. Reflecting on the incident, he expressed relief, stating, "Damn, I'm glad I didn't shoot the nigga."

In response, I emphasized the belief in a higher power, suggesting that it was perhaps divine intervention that caused the gun to malfunction.

I conveyed the idea that this fortunate outcome provided him with another opportunity to live life outside of prison.

Young Loc's incarceration stems from a murder incident at Dr. J's Liquor Store, a grim reality evidenced by a surveillance image he shared with me, capturing him in the act of firing a gun. Despite this, I hold onto hope as I anticipate my upcoming court appearance, praying for the chance to return to the streets.

Recently, G-Man, a fellow accomplice in my criminal endeavors, entered the cell block. Our last encounter involved counting stacks of cash obtained from ATMs. I had previously acquired a mini-14 from him, but relinquished it when I found myself in lockdown on this particular stint.

Reflecting on this, I believe my confinement was divinely orchestrated; it compelled me to dispose of all firearms I had stashed across the city.

Now, I stand on the precipice of transformation, having shed my past transgressions and endeavored to align my actions with the teachings of the Bible.

I'm feeling optimistic these days. No more confrontations with fellow inmates or deputies. I've immersed myself in the teachings of God, striving to love my brothers as I love myself and seeking forgiveness for my past actions. Hopefully, this transformation will bear fruit.

The Southsiders and I have held three Bible study sessions together, and I've noticed a shift in my demeanor. Instead of feeling combative, I'm more receptive to hearing others' testimonies about their lives.

It's like I've finally found some light in the darkness.

HC was transferred back to Vista, a move that brought him closer to his family, which he welcomed. Meanwhile, Blue Light has begun writing his book.

He approached me today, seeking advice on getting it published, revealing that he's already penned 17 pages. I encouraged him to keep going until he reaches 34 pages.

It's a first for someone to start a book based on my advice.

Tomorrow, I have a court date looming.

I haven't delved much into the details of my case, but here's the gist: I'm facing charges of kidnapping, kidnapping for robbery, false imprisonment, threatening to terrorize, and kidnapping with injury.

Facing an additional 50 years due to gang enhancement is a hefty burden to bear. Despite no longer being affiliated with any gang, the detective handling my case has woven a gang narrative into every aspect to strengthen his case against me.

Chapter 19

I KEPT MY FAITH IN GOD

The contents of the police report don't cast me as a criminal; rather, they illuminate my past as a gang member and leader.

This revelation has brought immense stress into my life.

Nonetheless, I believe that I've been placed here by God to serve as a warning to those considering gang involvement.

It's crucial for people to understand the grim reality of joining gangs and engaging in criminal activities.

Through this ordeal, I've experienced life both as a guilty and innocent man.

Throughout it all, my faith in God has remained steadfast. I cherish each day and vow to live it to the fullest.

Recently, Mike from the Logan Barrios, also known as Smokie, shared his life testimony with me.

He embarked on a similar journey, beginning in San Quentin during the early 80s.

Today, he offered his perspective and insights into the challenges and consequences of gang involvement. He could have been the one to pen this book, but fate chose me.

He confided, "D-Man, I've got murder in my heart. It's not the right time for me to come out." Despite facing a potential life sentence, he found solace in the fact that his son shared my name, Derek.

I reassured him, "Mike, I'm just like you."

Young Loc received a gift basket from his grandmother a testament to the enduring love of family for a grandson who remains dearly remembered.

As you get to know these individuals, you can't help but develop a profound affection for them, as long as you overcome any fear you may have.

All it takes is the love of God and the assurance that someone cares, as I do, for others to learn from their journeys. I attended court for my preliminary hearing a trial before the actual trial.

Of the five charges against me, three were dropped, which was a positive development, but there's still room for improvement.

Similarly, my co-defendant Al-Dog saw two charges dropped.

This serves as evidence that we weren't collaborating closely, otherwise, we'd be facing the same charges now.

As I sat in court, some of my friends and family members came to show their support, laughing and joking before I entered the courtroom.

The deputy warned me, "Grover, don't try to speak to anyone you know. If you do, I'll have to remove them from the courtroom."

Their chatter only grew louder behind me. Frustrated, I turned to the deputy and quipped, "Deputy, can you take me out of the courtroom now?"

He obliged, escorting me next to the Judge's chambers, where my attorney and Al-Dog's attorney were meeting with the D.A. and Judge. However, the victim of the case didn't appear, likely out of fear.

After court, I was returned to the court tanks, where I confronted the deputies who had choked me out and beaten me down. I demanded to know who had choked me out. Deputy King revealed, "It was a Sergeant."

I inquired, "Why did he do it?" He responded, "Because he thought you were fighting one of the deputies."

Deputy Lewis then asked me if I was okay with the inmates in the tank.

I assured him, "Yeah. I'm not going to fight anyone." He paused, opened the cell door, and pulled me out, asking, "What the fuck happened?"

I explained that I didn't want to go to court and had asked for help from the deputies at Bailey.

I confessed that I was inclined to hurt someone and needed assistance.

I disclosed my past as a gang leader and the battles I'd faced.

To prove my point, I mentioned my book, which they promptly looked up on the internet and brought me some paperwork on it. The other inmates watched in silence as this unfolded, three dozen of them.

FROM THE INSIDE LOOKING OUT

The events chronicled in this book are nonfiction, witnessed firsthand by the author, Derek Grover, during his time at the George Bailey Detention Facility in San Diego, CA.

Derek Grover is a battle-hardened former gang leader and crime boss, known for his authenticity and refusal to engage in pretense or imagination.

Books Available by Derek Grover

Fighting For Your LIFE INSIDE

Southern California's Most Notorious

Jails and Prisons

Also available

The Gangbangers Dictionary

Derek Grover has written this powerful and most informative book on gang affiliation. The book is Titled "The Gangbanger's Dictionary One Hundred and Eighty-seven things you better know before you join a gang.

This book will take its reader on a 25-year journey of gangbanging in the streets of Southeast San Diego.

About the author

Former gangster Derek Grover, also known as D-Man, rose to infamy as the leader and crime boss of the formidable Bloccide Crips street gang in Southeast San Diego. Engaged in numerous gunfights with rival gangsters and deadly shootouts with the San Diego Police, Grover now channels his experiences into his writing to delve into the mindset of a criminal street gang.

His books are crafted to resonate with gang members and those contemplating gang involvement, offering a perspective only someone who has lived it can provide. Grover has transitioned into a writer, author, and social activist, leveraging his understanding of the inner workings of a criminal street gang. Today, he dedicates his time to speaking engagements and lectures aimed at at-risk community members, educators, and youth, shedding light on the harsh realities of gang life and advocating for positive alternatives.

ONE EIGHTYSEVEN

A DAY IN THE LIFE

If these walls could talk, they would
echo the tales of gangsters locked in
a ceaseless battle of murder beefs and
internal strife. These stories unfold
within the confines of the George
Bailey Detention Facility in San Diego,
California, penned by Derek Grover,
also known as D-Man, a notorious figure
within the gang world. These are not
fictional narratives; they are raw, real-
life accounts of gangsters navigating
the perilous streets, written by one who
has lived through it all.

Printed in the United States
by Baker & Taylor Publisher Services